Welcome to the EVERYTHING® series!

THESE HANDY, accessible books give you all you need to tackle a difficult project, gain a new hobby, comprehend a fascinating topic, prepare for an exam, or even brush up on something you learned back in school but have since forgotten.

You can read an *EVERYTHING*® book from cover-to-cover or just pick out the information you want from our four useful boxes: e-facts, e-ssentials, e-alerts, and e-questions. We literally give you everything you need to know on the subject, but throw in a lot of fun stuff along the way, too.

We now have well over 100 *EVERYTHING*® books in print, spanning such wide-ranging topics as weddings, pregnancy, wine, learning guitar, one-pot cooking, managing people, and so much more. When you're done reading them all, you can finally say you know *EVERYTHING*®!

 Ⓔ **FACTS:** Important sound bytes of information

 Ⓔ **ESSENTIALS:** Quick and handy tips

 Ⓔ **ALERTS!:** Urgent warnings

 Ⓔ **QUESTIONS:** Solutions to common problems

THE

EVERYTHING

— Series —

Dear Reader,

I love weddings—there's nothing more wonderful than seeing two people making a commitment—and I love helping to plan weddings. I also love to save money—it's disheartening for me to see so many brides and grooms feeling pressured to spend, spend, spend. This is a time when they should be encouraged to be careful with money and not overextend themselves in any way!

Some people don't believe that the two things can be compatible. They think that if you're planning a wedding, you're about to go into serious debt. Not true! It's possible to have a lovely wedding on far less money than you'd imagine. Even if you have a significant budget, you want to spend your money wisely.

Maybe you want to focus on one specific element of the wedding and find savings in other areas. Maybe you want to save whatever you can for a down payment on a house or a dream honeymoon. Maybe you're like some of us who just don't like to see money wasted.

I hope you'll use this book to better plan your wedding and honeymoon. Have a wonderful wedding and a wonderful life together!

Barbara Cameron

THE EVERYTHING

WEDDINGS ON A BUDGET BOOK

Create the wedding of your dreams and have money left for the honeymoon

Barbara Cameron

Adams Media Corporation
Avon, Massachusetts

An Everything® Series Book.
Everything® and everything.com® are registered trademarks
of F+W Publications, Inc.

Published by Adams Media, an F+W Publications Company
57 Littlefield Street, Avon, MA 02322 U.S.A.
www.adamsmedia.com

ISBN: 1-58062-782-X
Printed in Canada.

J I H G F E D C B

Library of Congress Cataloging-in-Publication Data
Cameron, Barbara.
The everything weddings on a budget book : create the wedding of your
dreams and have money left for the honeymoon / Barbara Cameron.
p.   cm.   (An everything series book)
Includes index.
ISBN 1-58062-782-X
1. Weddings–Planning. 2. Wedding etiquette. 3. Budgets, Personal.
I. Title. II. Everything series.
HQ745 .C35 2002
395.2'2–dc21
2002009370

This publication is designed to provide accurate and authoritative information with regard to the subject matter covered. It is sold with the understanding that the publisher is not engaged in rendering legal, accounting,
or other professional advice. If legal advice or other expert assistance is
required, the services of a competent professional person should be sought.
—From a *Declaration of Principles* jointly adopted by a
Committee of the American Bar Association and
a Committee of Publishers and Associations

Illustrations by Barry Littmann.

*This book is available at quantity discounts for bulk purchases.
For information, call 1-800-872-5627.*

Visit the entire Everything® series at everything.com

THE

EVERYTHING
Series

EDITORIAL

Publishing Director: Gary M. Krebs
Managing Editor: Kate McBride
Copy Chief: Laura MacLaughlin
Acquisitions Editor: Kate Epstein
Development Editors: Julie Gutin, Christel A. Shea
Production Editor: Khrysti Nazzaro

PRODUCTION

Production Director: Susan Beale
Production Manager: Michelle Roy Kelly
Series Designer: Daria Perreault
Cover Design: Paul Beatrice and Frank Rivera
Layout and Graphics: Colleen Cunningham,
Rachael Eiben, Michelle Roy Kelly,
Daria Perreault

Contents

Introduction

CONGRATULATIONS on your engagement and on being a wise consumer! Being in love and planning the wedding and honeymoon of your dreams is emotional and exciting. It's a time when you feel like spending whatever it takes to have what you want.

That's exactly how the people in the wedding business are hoping you're feeling! There are hundreds of businesses, books, magazines, Web sites, and more out there, just waiting to tell you all the things you need and how much you will have to spend for them. Although there are many wonderful and trustworthy wedding professionals out there, you will also find those who would take advantage—just like in any other type of business.

Everyone wants to get the most for their money these days, and your wedding and honeymoon shouldn't be any different. The fact that you've picked up *The Everything® Weddings on a Budget Book* is proof that you want to be careful and wise with the planning of your wedding, your honeymoon, and your future. Good for you!

This book will show you how to be a smart consumer so you and your fiancé don't overspend and start your new life together with financial problems. Now, you might feel that being asked to think about money—and how to save it—all the time might take the fun, romance, and excitement out of planning the most important event of your life.

We think that feeling taken advantage of and going broke *will* take the romance out of things.

That's why *The Everything® Weddings on a Budget Book* is exactly what you need. It'll help you decide on what type of budget will work for you, and help you plan and spend wisely to have that wedding and honeymoon of your dreams. You don't have to feel as though being on a budget means that you are skimping or settling for second best. A budget is simply a thought-out plan for spending wisely, whether it's for hundreds of dollars, or hundreds of thousands of dollars.

Today, most couples and their families and friends have busy, busy lives. They're already squeezing forty-eight hours of activity into twenty-four-hour days, and no one has the time to run around and investigate a dozen stores to save money. Even the participants who enjoy making things don't have the time they used to and have to find shortcuts.

The Everything® Weddings on a Budget Book includes ways to save time as well as ways to save money because time truly is money for most of us. After all, you want to have a life while you're planning the events that launch the life you and your fiancé have together. Wedding and honeymoon planning can't be all that you do and think about for the months ahead!

Think of a budget as the best way to get exactly what you want for exactly what you want to spend. That way, you'll have more money, time, and energy for that honeymoon after the wedding. You deserve it!

The Everything® Weddings on a Budget Book is filled with the practical advice and suggestions of many brides, their friends, relatives, and parents, as well as wedding professionals. They give specifics of what they learned about how to have the wedding and honeymoon of their dreams. With their help, you too can make your wedding and honeymoon dreams come true!

CHAPTER 1
Making a Budget

You've seen those articles in magazines and newspapers reporting that the "average" wedding costs a certain figure these days. Oh, really? Maybe when you add into the average the outrageous amounts spent by celebrities. *You* choose the amount that is appropriate for your budget and then find ways to make your special day priceless.

Budget Is a Good Word

What's a budget, you ask? If you've never put together a budget plan, let alone stuck to one, this chapter is crucial to your financial health, both in preparation for your wedding and for years to come!

A Budget: Defined

First, a quick and simple definition of a budget—just so we're on the same page, so to speak. Webster defines the word as a plan for the coordination of resources (as of money or manpower) and expenditures, especially such a plan covering a definite period of time or the amount of money available or assigned to a particular purpose (Webster's *Third New International Dictionary*, 1993).

Perhaps you already keep a monthly budget, planning for living expenses and also budgeting for the unexpected—car repairs, that business suit that goes on sale for half price, and so on. A wedding budget is very similar—a plan for expected and unexpected expenditures.

 ESSENTIAL

Think about the sense of satisfaction and accomplishment you'll feel if you set a budget and "bring in" the wedding expenses within that budget. It's a good skill to learn for daily living within your paycheck, and for making big purchases like that future home or a new car.

So if you're a budgeter, you'll feel at home with the process—and if you're a first-timer, this may be the start of a new way of looking at how you spend.

It's Not Just about Money

Money is a topic fraught with potential emotional issues and stress. How you and your fiancé plan for the first expenses of your life together will set the stage for harmony in your relationship. There will never be a time when it is more important to make a realistic budget without emptying out the checking account, maxing out your credit cards, or, if they're paying, making either set of parents upset.

The First Step

Knowing what each one of you wants is the first step to planning your wedding. Grab your fiancé, find a comfortable seat, and take this easy quiz together. It'll help the two of you to determine your budget and prepare a better plan for that special day.

Your Budget

You know you're perfect for each other over the long haul, but what did you discover after taking the wedding-planning quiz? Were your ideas and dreams for the wedding alike, or did they seem miles apart? Certainly even the most compatible couple can have widely varying visions of what their wedding day should be and how much it should cost. Whether you have different expectations based on the wedding you've always imagined, or different priorities due to your plans for the future, be prepared for wedding planning to require communication and compromise.

PLAN YOUR WEDDING: A QUIZ

1. Where do you want to hold the wedding ceremony?

   a. church
   b. outdoor location (such as a park)
   c. home
   d. destination wedding
   e. mansion or a historical site
   f. other: _____

2. Where do you want to hold the reception?

   a. church hall
   b. hotel
   c. resort
   d. fellowship hall or community center
   e. other: _____

3. How many people will you invite?

   a. 5–25
   b. 25–50
   c. 50–100
   d. 100+

4. How much can you spend on the wedding and reception?

   a. $1–$2,000
   b. $2,001–$10,000
   c. $10,001–$20,000
   d. $20,000+

5. Who will pay for the wedding and reception?

   a. bride's parents
   b. groom's parents
   c. bride and groom's parents
   d. bride and groom

6. If you will pay for all or part of the wedding, how will you pay for it?

   a. savings
   b. loan
   c. by credit card
   d. a combination of savings, loans, and
      credit cards

7. What tasks will you do for the wedding?

   a. ceremony planning
   b. reception planning
   c. invitations
   d. decorations, favors, gifts

PLAN YOUR WEDDING: A QUIZ (continued)

e. music
f. transportation
g. food, cake, beverages
h. budgeting
i. photography
j. wedding Web site
k. honeymoon plans
l. other: _____

8. How much will you spend on a honeymoon?

a. $1–$1,000
b. $1,001–$3,000
c. $3,000+

9. Where will you go for a honeymoon?

a. someplace exotic in the United States
b. bed-and-breakfast in the United States
c. the Caribbean
d. big city in the United States or overseas
e. a nature destination
f. other: _____

10. What types of things do you need to register for to set up your new home?

a. household items
b. bed and bath items

c. electronic gifts (television, microwave, stereo, camera, etc.)

d. honeymoon registry

e. other: _____

■ ■ ■

So, how did you do? Once the two of you can figure out what you want and how you envision your wedding, you can begin to plan all the details—including, of course, the budget.

What Did the Quiz Reveal?

What kind of results did you get from taking the quiz together? Were there any surprises? Did one of you want to get married in a church and the other prefer an outdoor setting? Did one want your minister to perform the ceremony and the other want a nonreligious officiant?

And, perhaps even more importantly, did you discover major differences between the total amounts you each want to spend, or in the way that you want to pay for your wedding day? Perhaps one of you wants to have a big fancy wedding and when money runs out use a credit card, an idea that makes the other person look ready to faint.

Such differences in opinion are easier to overcome than you might think. By making a budget, you can then find ways to save money on certain items or services that you'll then be able to spend on the things that are more important to you.

Decide Now What's Most Important

Ask yourselves which of the features of the wedding are important to you. Each of you should make a list, and then star the two or three that are the most important. Is it the ceremony itself? The reception afterward? The wedding dress? Flowers? Think about it.

Now, compare your two lists. How closely do you and your fiancé agree on the big expenditures? Which two or three features mattered most to you? Let's say for you it's the dress and flowers and reception. For him, it's the reception and the music. Now you know how and where you'll want to focus money and time within your budget.

 FACT

Approximately 50 percent of the total wedding budget will be for the wedding attire, flowers, ceremony expenses, the photographer, and the videographer, if you use one. The reception can cost up to the remaining 50 percent.

Putting Your Heads Together

Now it's time to get together with those involved in footing the bill for the wedding and reception. Is the bride's family paying, or is the groom's? Are you essentially paying for it yourselves? Many couples are older and financially secure enough to pay for their own wedding—today, there are no rules for who pays!

Are There Strings on the Money?

If your family is paying, what will be the amount of the wedding budget? Is it the maximum, or can there be an adjustment if something unforeseen happens? Will the money be put into an account to draw on, or will you make up a payment schedule for expenditures? Obviously, if family members are paying the majority of your expenses, you must exercise diplomacy and responsibility.

Remember that when others are helping foot the bill, they may feel that they have something to say about how the money is spent. You and your fiancé will have to carefully consider the "hidden costs" of accepting money if you feel there may be problems. Your wedding—and planning it—is supposed to be a joyous occasion—not one fraught with controversy and conflict. You may have to "choose your battles," in a sense. If there are ongoing disagreements, decide what you absolutely must have, and weigh it against having the financial help—you may find that some things aren't as important as you thought!

 ESSENTIAL

Estimates vary, but between one-third and one-half of couples pay for their wedding themselves. Some couples prefer it, because they are able to make all decisions about the wedding themselves—without conflicts that might arise from others contributing to the wedding budget.

If you and your fiancé will be paying for your wedding, how will you make it work? Will you set up a joint account just for the wedding (recommended), or will you make the payments and deposits as needed and divide them?

Three Budget Categories

All couples have different financial resources and different types of expectations of how their wedding should be. That said, it's still important that you get a feel for some general guidelines. Follow three couples as they plan budgets that can be considered modest, moderate, and luxurious.

A Modest Budget

Amanda and her fiancé, Dustin, are planning a modest wedding. It will be a small and intimate wedding, with two dozen friends and family members. Together, they have established a goal of saving on the wedding expenses so that they can put a down payment on a house in the near future. They also hope to pay off their student loans.

In spite of their longer-term financial goals, there's no need for Amanda and Dustin to feel that they are compromising on the quality of their wedding. According to Amanda, "When it really comes down to it, Dustin and I don't want a lavish wedding. We'll just have those people who are really special with us on our wedding day." They'd like to hold their expenses down to under $1,000. Theirs is a modest budget.

A Moderate Budget

Tammie's parents are working with a budget of approximately $10,000 for her wedding, and Matt's parents may pick up a few of the "traditional" expenses as well. Nevertheless, the couple is staying conscious of expenses—they don't want their parents to feel strained. Let's call their budget moderate.

A Luxurious (Splurge) Wedding

JoEllen and her fiancé, Ben, have been living together and sharing expenses for the past two years, and they command high salaries as stockbrokers at a Wall Street firm. Together, JoEllen and Ben have set up a checking account with $25,000 designated for wedding expenses.

"We want to celebrate our wedding day with a big party and invite all our friends and some business associates," JoEllen explained. "Our jobs are dynamic and our days are long, so I'm hiring a wedding consultant to help me plan the wedding. We're pulling out all the stops to have a lavish, elegant day." JoEllen and Ben's budget may be called luxurious.

 FACT

You've just met three very different couples—all of which want to have the wedding of their dreams, just like you! Which couple has the most typical wedding budget? The average wedding in the United States ranges between $19,000 and $23,000.

Is Your Budget Modest, Moderate, or Luxurious?

First, sit down and decide how much you can spend. That's your bottom figure. Then decide how much you could stretch that if you had to, or if you discovered something that you realized you just had to have. Your budget must also include a substantial cushion to cover any miscellaneous or unexpected expenses.

Given your own ideas of how much money is "a lot," as well as what you've read in magazines or heard from friends, determine which category your budget falls into: modest, moderate, or luxurious.

Of course, what these categories really mean will be different depending on which part of the country you're in and the locale of your wedding. For example, a budget some would consider moderate could be termed modest in a larger, more expensive city. However, you may find it easier to locate items you need for your less expensive wedding within the wide variety of options larger cities offer. Small towns may have only one vendor for a wedding gown, and one photographer. So, you may incur additional expenses for travel time—either because you have to drive to a bigger city to find what you want, or because you choose more distant vendors to come to you.

Tips for Budget Success

Perhaps you've heard the "statistic" that one-half of all marriages in this country end in divorce. Well, other experts debate that divorce statistic, saying that you don't take the marriages made in one year and subtract all divorces that year and come up with a "fact" that half of all marriages fail. However, few experts debate the fact that most people report money problems as being the cause of their relationship failures.

 ALERT!

If you're afraid that you're in a high, happy mood because you're engaged and planning to marry that special person and you might spend too much, leave your checkbook or credit card locked in your car. You'll avoid impulse purchases if you have to walk out to the car to retrieve them.

Why is this important to you as you make your wedding budget? Think about your wedding budget as one of the first places that you and your fiancé will discuss your attitudes about money, plan expenditures, and work together to plan your marriage. It's the perfect place to start out on the right way to a successful marriage. Even if one of you is doing most of the planning and spending, it's important that you both agree on how this will be done. And that spirit of budgetary responsibility will reflect itself in marital harmony.

Watch out for Money Pitfalls

While money is unarguably the biggest source of disagreement between married couples, the real issue is not how much money you have, but the way you reach an agreement on how you will spend it. Marriage counselors will tell you that they've had very, very wealthy couples who have lots of money but still fight about who spends how much on what.

Making your financial decisions—for the wedding and for life—through discussion, compromise, and sound budget principles will set you up for success. Apply these principles not only to your wedding expenses, but also throughout your financial future together.

What Is Your Money Personality?

You can guarantee budget success—and a happy money relationship—with your fiancé if you think about the types of money personalities the two of you have.

Is either of you impulsive? Does a bad or stressful day at the office drive you to frivolous spending at the mall? Do you feel that you work hard and deserve to have what you want?

Or is one of you excessively frugal? Do you find it hard to spend money, and give every potential purchase so much thought that others squirm when they're out shopping with you?

Neither extreme is good, and if one of you is an impulsive spender and the other is painfully frugal, this combination can spell disaster for financial decisions you make as a couple.

FACT

> Always ask if you qualify for a discount. Most people know about discounts for senior citizens (and some companies begin that discount at age fifty), but there are often discounts for students, those who work for certain businesses and professions, AAA members, repeat customers, and so on.

What Is Your Spending Style?

Your spending styles are determined by what you observed growing up. If there were fights over money in your family, you may have formed the idea that certain spending styles are bad. Such experiences will lead you to make financial decisions accordingly, and you may be critical of others who have different spending styles. Maybe there were no fights over money in your family (really? Wow!). In that case, perhaps you've developed a healthy attitude about money and you will carry that into your own marriage.

Personal Stories

"My parents are divorced," recounts Amanda, "and I can remember hearing a lot of arguments about money. I don't want that with Dustin, so we've done a lot of talking about how we'll deal with money issues when we're married. We're not going to get into a lot of debt to get married—partly because we want a house within the next year or two, and partly because we feel like we've already gotten into a lot of debt getting our college degrees. We hope we'll have good jobs very soon, but we do want to be careful."

Tammie's parents have a long-lasting marriage and are co-owners of a business. They make money decisions in both their marriage and their business with ease. Matt's parents often disagreed about how money would be spent. However, he saw them find ways to compromise. Both Tammie and Matt feel that their parents have been good role models for how couples should handle money.

 QUESTION?

How can you prevent impulsive purchases or financial commitments?
Before making a purchase for your wedding—especially the big-ticket items like a wedding dress—ask yourself if you really *need* the item, or if you just *want* it. Make it a rule to think about it overnight, see how you feel the next day, and then make your decision.

JoEllen reports that she often heads to the mall or tunes in to the TV shopping channels when she's had an unusually tiring and stressful day. She has had to consciously work on not making impulsive purchases.

"Ben tends to make impulsive purchases, too, but it

happens more because he sees a good deal, not because he's stressed," JoEllen says. "I don't think either of us makes decisions about money based on how our parents handled money issues. I think it's more that we have to have a faster-paced way of making money decisions given our careers and the work that we do."

JoEllen also knows that despite having the money for a lavish wedding set aside, expenses can get out of control if she falls into her habitual patterns of spending impulsively when she's tired and stressed.

CHAPTER 2

Carrying out Your Plans

Now that you know what you want and what you can afford, you need to create a plan of how you will convert your wishes to reality. This chapter will get you started, and the subsequent chapters will help you deal with particular issues in greater detail.

Getting Started

You have so many things to remember as you plan for your wedding, you might be feeling overwhelmed. This list of what you might need will be helpful—if only to get you to start thinking!

Regardless of whether you are planning a modest, moderate, or luxurious wedding, you'll need to account for the basics. Typical planned expenditures include:

❑ Invitations, and other printed materials such as the wedding program
❑ Bride's wedding gown, alterations, and accessories
❑ Groom's attire
❑ Flowers (bouquets, wedding and reception location flowers, corsages for the mothers and grandmothers, boutonnieres, etc.)
❑ Ceremony location
❑ Reception (location and food)
❑ Music
❑ Photography (and video, if desired)
❑ Transportation
❑ Wedding rings
❑ Marriage license
❑ Blood tests (if required)
❑ Officiant's fee
❑ Wedding party gifts
❑ Rehearsal dinner
❑ Lodging for out-of-town family and guests (optional)
❑ Honeymoon

ESSENTIAL

If yours is a traditional wedding like Tammie and Matt's, the groom's family may pay for certain expenses such as the marriage license, wedding officiant's fee, the bride's bouquet and going-away corsage, the rehearsal dinner, the honeymoon, and some lodging expenses.

The Big Two

Typically, the two most important factors of wedding expenditures are size and location. Begin the planning process by asking the following two questions:

- How many guests did you decide on? Since the reception often costs up to one-half of the final cost of the wedding, knowing the number of guests you have to plan for is crucial right from the beginning.
- Where will the wedding and reception take place? Wedding and reception venues vary widely in price, so narrowing (or nailing down!) your choices as soon as possible is essential for budgeting and planning.

ALERT!

The size of the party and the location of the wedding will require the biggest part of your wedding budget and will make a difference in how much money you have left over for other expenses, like your wedding gown or the photographer.

During the months of planning, it will be important to stick to a set number of guests and not let the guest list mushroom, because that will make your total expenses rise in direct proportion. For more details on how to pick the site of your wedding ceremony, see Chapter 3.

Budget Your Time

An important part of laying out a plan for yourself is to budget your time. Time really is money—worth money, that is! Sure, you could save money by doing most things for your wedding yourself. But do you really want to be up late the night before your ceremony affixing flowers to a wedding canopy, writing out a seating chart, and folding napkins into swans? Not only will you look stressed and haggard the next day, you will *feel* it, and you'll really miss out on enjoying the perfect experience that you've both worked so hard to create.

Keeping in mind all you have to do, it may be worth the financial investment to have as many arrangements and details and things as possible taken care of by others. Really, it's a basic strategy of delegation.

Then, too, the better your time is organized, the more of it you will have to spend looking for bargains and arranging realistic delivery dates. No one wants to hear that charges are doubled because last-minute orders require surcharges for express delivery or extra manpower. Making a time budget—and keeping it in a prominent place—will save time and money. (You can use Appendix B, "Time Budget Worksheet," to keep track of your time budget.)

QUESTION?

What are the benefits to registering online?
A better question is, what are the drawbacks? Because it's hard to find any. You can each browse on your own before trying to make your list together. You can change your lists. You can even access stores that aren't available in your area but may be convenient to your guests.

Get Online

Logging on to the Internet may be the biggest single money and time saver of all. There are thousands of

Web sites with advice and suggestions, ranging from those of the bridal magazines to sites set up by recently married couples eager to share with other couples what worked and what didn't.

Whether you live in a big city or a small town, there is an incredible wealth of sites offering information on all the different services and items you will need. Use search engines to find wedding locations in the area you're considering. Skimming through the listed sites can make selecting locations a breeze—you can usually view the facilities and eliminate many options that way.

You may also find many Web sites maintained by wedding location specialists, from private entrepreneurs to local and state agencies in charge of parks, civic sites, and so on. You'll save the time and money required to drive all over or make phone calls, and you'll also save yourself frazzled nerves! Sites such as eBay are increasingly popular for finding bargains, including wedding dresses, veils, wedding party clothes, tuxedoes for the groom and his party, accessories, and more.

E-Mail, Not Snail Mail

You probably already keep in touch with friends and family via e-mail—now you can save a lot of hassle by using e-mail to let them know about your wedding planning and send photos of dresses, locations, and so on.

QUESTION?

> **How can working online make planning a wedding easier?**
> It's possible to save a lot of time and money by using the Internet, whether you use it to purchase goods and services, or just to investigate what's out there for your wedding and how much it might cost.

Wedding Consultants

Another big time saver—and, in some cases, a money saver—is to hire a wedding consultant. Some consultants charge a flat fee; others charge a percentage of the wedding budget (typically 10 to 15 percent). Be sure to clarify fees before you make a final decision about the person you're thinking of hiring and working with, but don't make your decision based on the fee alone. Consider how much you plan on having the consultant do for you. Keep in mind that good consultants often have working relationships with excellent vendors and venues, and those connections may translate into opportunities for savings.

What Can You Do for Me?

Time is probably the most important thing that a wedding consultant can save you. Most couples work these days, as do their parents, and even grandparents. You may not have the time to plan the wedding the way you'd like, and you may not have people in your circle of family or friends who can help you.

What about Experience?

Ask your potential wedding consultants about their experience. Some people take special courses; others use the term to loosely describe themselves, when actually they only want to sell you their very own goods or services. Depending, again, on the amount of work you'll have the consultant do for you, you may not need someone with professional training, so be clear on what services you actually need.

Similarly, some wedding consultants provide rental items for a wedding and reception, such as the candleholders, chairs, vases, and so on. Do some comparison-shopping to price out these items so you know that you're not being overcharged.

 ESSENTIAL

> Look at the Sample Budget Worksheet at the back of the book (Appendix A) when you are ready to begin working up your budget. Don't worry—help is at hand in every chapter!

Whether you choose a "wedding services provider" or an actual consultant, be sure you get a list of references—and *call them*! Talk to former clients and find out, first, if the consultant did all she was supposed to do. But also take the time to get a feel for the person you are talking to so you can determine if the consultant will also provide the style and quality of service you want.

Always remember to fully examine the claims of any so-called wedding consultant. Ask your friends for the names of consultants they've used or can recommend. The most important thing, again, is to ask the consultant about his or her experience, and don't be afraid to ask for references and check them out!

Other Solutions Are out There

If you don't hire a wedding consultant, remember that reception sites such as hotels also have events planners who can help a great deal in planning your wedding and reception. There'll be more on other helpful people in coming chapters, too!

Saving Money May Require Unusual Methods

In preparation for your wedding, you need to keep in mind that many services offered don't have set prices—they are open for discussion. If you've never bargained with a salesperson or vendor—perhaps you've thought that haggling is distasteful—now may be the time for you to learn that it's an acceptable practice and can be beneficial for all involved. Often, vendors would rather compromise on a price than lose the sale.

How you approach a vendor can mean the difference

between success and failure. For example, ask the florist if you can get a discount for placing the order and putting down a deposit six months in advance. You could also offer to have a friend pick up the cake to save on a delivery fee, if that's an option.

A Novel Idea

Recently, some couples have been offering to put the names of their vendors on the backs of their wedding programs in exchange for free goods, services, or a concession in price. They pay next to nothing for their wedding day in exchange for some "advertising."

 FACT

> There's a fine line between advertising and being tacky—don't cross it. A personal thank-you to certain vendors on the back of your program is subtle, yet effective. A full-page spread that announces the name of your wedding gown designer is not.

Protect Yourself

Remember to get everything in writing. You don't want to have to put down additional deposits when you find that your arrangements fall through. Don't rely on verbal assurances—too much is at stake!

Putting big purchases on a credit card is also important. First and foremost, you will have more consumer recourse if something goes wrong than if you pay with a check. Second, you may also reap the benefits of points, air miles, or other promotional programs. Your honeymoon is the perfect opportunity to take advantage of such perks, so call your credit card company and see what they have available. Be sure to read the terms and conditions thoroughly. In order for this money-saving measure to work, you absolutely must pay the card's balance in full each month.

Timing Is Everything

You may be able to save a significant amount of money if you have the flexibility to schedule your wedding (or even just the honeymoon) during the off-peak season. Vendors may be willing to negotiate with you for lower rental fees for chairs, tents, and so on. You will also enjoy less crowded conditions at wedding and honeymoon venues.

As you plan your date—and keeping your guest list in mind—ask yourselves how important the month and even the day of the week are to you. If you are having a small wedding and most of your guests are local, a Friday evening or Sunday afternoon wedding could work well. Remember that as long as you are within your budget, what you save on one factor can be put toward another!

Chapter 3

The Wedding Ceremony

Have you made the decision on where you want to have your wedding ceremony? Here's hoping you haven't, because there are some wonderful ways to get the place that you want within your budget. Even if your dream seems unattainable in terms of cost or location, you can incorporate elements of that dream into the reality of your big day.

Make a Date—and Set One!

First, make a date with your fiancé to sit down and talk about where to have your ceremony. Set aside a few hours one evening or sometime during the weekend, and together list some of the possible places for a wedding. Perhaps there are some that you haven't thought of, and this time together can serve as a way to inspire you to investigate them as potential candidates for the perfect place for your special day.

The Ceremony Site Starts It All

Couples should talk about where they want to have the wedding ceremony first because it will dictate everything else—the bride and groom's attire, where to hold the reception, transportation needs, decorations, and so many other details!

Some couples want to have both the wedding and the reception in the same place. They don't want a big gap in their day, especially since there may be some time spent on taking photographs after the wedding, which will slow things down. Then again, the location may simply lend itself to having both parts of the day there.

If, however, you want to be married in a religious ceremony in a church, synagogue, or other place of worship, and there is a reason why you don't want to have the reception there, that's fine, too. For more on choosing particular reception sites, see Chapter 4.

What's Most Important?

By now you have an idea of what type of wedding budget you will have. Perhaps you have a modest budget but you wanted the moderate or even the luxurious one. Think of that one special element that you just wish you could have but don't have the money for. Don't give it up yet! Let's rethink your options.

By this point in your life, you've probably attended several weddings and observed (and critiqued!) even more on television and at the movies. What do you really remember about those you've attended? Although everyone remembers different things, for most it was the special mood of the day, the way the bride and groom looked at each other, and just one detail that, while not necessarily large, really seemed significant.

 ALERT!

> If you are worried about all the decisions you have to make and how much money you need to spend, remember that in the end, it's all about how happy—not stressed!—the two of you are on your wedding day.

So Many Ideas!

Many couples choose to have a traditional ceremony in a church or a synagogue. Sometimes they're an active member or frequent attendee, and they can't think of any place more appropriate. Other couples who don't necessarily attend a place of worship on a regular basis still want to be married in a religious setting. Perhaps it has always been done in their family, and they find themselves looking for a place of religious significance for their wedding day.

However, a wedding ceremony can be just as spiritual—as meaningful and solemn—in a nontraditional setting. Once you start looking at alternative places for your ceremony, you may find that the savings over a formal church or synagogue wedding can be significant in some cases.

"We wanted to get married in my church, but were surprised by how expensive it was going to be," said one bride. "It's a large church, and its usage fee is based on that. But we will be inviting only a hundred guests, and we have a limited budget."

How about Outdoors?

Upon discovering that a church wedding would blow their budget, one couple looked into having a ceremony in a different location. An outdoor location appealed to the groom-to-be, so one afternoon he surprised his fiancée with a picnic lunch and a list of sites he thought would be perfect. They looked them over, and then ate lunch in a little park beside a beautiful river—the place he secretly liked best but wanted to see her reaction to. She loved it, and her minister was happy to marry the couple there.

Of course, outdoor locations abound. There are

beautiful parks located in nearly every community, many with pavilions or gazebos or other special structures that make for a truly lovely ceremony. If you live near the ocean, you can get married on the beach as dawn breaks or the sun sets.

 ESSENTIAL

Outdoor locations can be less expensive than a church or synagogue setting, but some are tricky. Do you have a backup plan if the weather is bad? Is the terrain easy to walk on? What kind of permits do you have to get from local authorities? How much do they cost? Will you need to rent outdoor restroom facilities?

One couple met during the summer while performing a state historic play on an outdoor stage in St. Augustine, Florida. "We'd sit and hold hands in the moonlight and talk after the play each night. The following year, we were married on that same stage. The whole audience—with our friends and family there, of course—was invited to stay after the performance for the ceremony. We saved so much money, and friends said it was the most unusual wedding!"

Some couples meet while attending college, and so getting married in the college chapel or outdoors in a special spot where they met or studied together can be memorable. More and more couples are finding that getting married there feels "just right" and is the fitting transition to a new life together.

Make Your Own History

Historic mansions or plantations can be elegant sites; they are often so beautifully furnished and landscaped that they require little decoration for the ceremony. Not every town can boast a Biltmore Plantation, but there are many likely homes that are lovely and have historic status. There may be a historic inn, lighthouse, or pier that would make a unique setting for your wedding.

 FACT

Individuals other than ministers or rabbis can officiate at your wedding. Your county courthouse will have information on how to become an officiant for a specific date or event. Even if you don't save money over the cost of a minister or rabbi, the honor of having a friend or family member marry you will be priceless.

How about an Artful Place?

Museums and cultural centers make lovely sites for weddings, too, with their displays of artwork and elegant decorations. Casual wedding sites include beaches, some parks, even country-western clubs where you, your new spouse, and your guests can do the two-step afterward.

Visit some locations together. If you find an outdoor location you like, sit in it for a while and see if you feel the kind of mood you want for your wedding. Is it quiet enough? How might the location be in the season or time of day you want?

Consider These Locations

For a truly elegant ceremony site, what about a civic center, or a marina or country club? Disney World in Orlando, Florida, offers a variety of wedding services in their many themed hotels, with the added bonus of fun and adventurous honeymoon options right there in the theme parks. It's a stateside destination location that may also appeal to the families and guests of the wedding couple, particularly if children will be attending.

Riverboats that traverse the Mississippi or a river near you are also hot spots for weddings. Couples may choose to reserve an entire cruise or just a portion of it. A unique bonus: The captain can perform the ceremony!

Want more locations that may save you money? Some cities have small chapels where you can get a package deal. One Lake Tahoe chapel offers several packages, with an economy wedding for $199, including the marriage license, filing, and a notary on site. Adding items such as more elaborate flowers, more chapel time, videography, and so on will increase the price. The most expensive package tops out at $1,195; it includes three hours in a stretch limousine.

ESSENTIAL

> Bed-and-breakfasts, inns, vineyards, and other similar locations offer opportunities for an elegant wedding ceremony for varying prices. Check out the prices for those in your area.

If either of you has interests such as Renaissance fairs or historical re-enactments, you may want to get married in period costumes you can make or may already have. Do some research to see if you can get married at these sites for little expense. Imagine the effect of having your marriage ceremony conducted by someone dressed as a king or a military captain. Again, items such as flowers and other decorations can be downplayed not only for savings but also because they wouldn't be historically accurate to the period.

Questions for Ceremony Site Coordinators

There are some important questions you'll need to ask the coordinator of the ceremony site in which you're interested:

1. What dates are available?
2. What is the fee? Does the fee change depending on the requested time of day or day of the week? When do we need to put down our deposit?

3. What are the seating options? Do we need to rent chairs and other items for the ceremony?

4. How long can we have the site? (You don't want to feel rushed.)

5. When can our florist arrive to decorate? Who will be here early to open the facility?

6. Are there any restrictions on decorating? (Some churches won't allow you to take your altar flowers when you leave; some won't allow candles because of concerns about fires.)

7. Is there an attached reception hall in case we decide to use it? What is the fee? What are the cleaning costs?

8. Can we bring in our own caterer if we want? What about alcohol?

9. For an outdoor location: Where can we move the wedding if it rains?

10. Is there a place for the wedding party to get dressed?

When considering both the questions and the answers, be sure you are both clear in what your first priority is. Your priorities may change as your plans come together, but be sure you know where you're willing to compromise so you don't end up with a facility that doesn't meet your most important needs and criteria.

No Place Like Home?

Homes have been used for weddings for hundreds of

years and are becoming more popular with couples who want a smaller, more intimate wedding with fewer guests, where the bride and groom can feel comfortable and cherished.

Savings Begin at Home

Savings can also be considerable when the ceremony is held at home. You don't have to budget for the usage or rental fee of a church or synagogue, and there's no cleaning fee, no decorations (after all, your home is already furnished), no transportation expenses incurred by running to a church and then a reception, and so on. (How to save on having parties at home will be covered in Chapter 13.)

Childhood Dreams Come True

"I dreamed of walking down our staircase to meet my husband-to-be from the first time I saw my family home as a little girl," a friend once confided. "I used to practice walking down the steps, holding a feather duster and pretending it was my bouquet. My mom and dad were thrilled when I asked if my fiancé and I could be married there. We stood before the fireplace and exchanged vows."

Ceremonies at home could also take place around a sparkling swimming pool or in a corner of a lovely garden. Even if the garden isn't the prettiest, it can be inexpensively fixed up with candles and pots of flowers from the local discount florist.

It Doesn't Have to Be Your Home

Consider asking a friend if you can get married at his or her house if it's someplace that you really love. Most people will feel flattered. Olivia estimated that she saved $400 on ceremony expenses and had a wedding that was even more special because she decided to have a home wedding.

 ALERT!

If you decide to have a home wedding, don't waste your savings by buying new furniture or drapes. The guests won't be focusing on your home—they'll be too busy looking at the bride and groom!

"A friend of mine had a big Victorian home that she knew I just loved," she said. "When I asked if Mark and I could be married there, she cried. We planted some flowers for the backyard ceremony and she said that now, when she looks at them, she remembers that day, and she's happy."

Olivia figures she saved an additional $500 because she automatically limited her guest list due to the smaller size of the house, and the fact that she didn't have to order expensive floral decorations for the church and reception site. Much of the catering was also done at the home.

Three Budget Examples

Amanda and Dustin were sitting together at their favorite spot on campus one day, talking about where they wanted to get married.

"It was so peaceful there. The alumni association gave the college money to make this big reflecting pool, and flowers were blooming and a little family of ducks was out on the water. We just looked at each other and thought, how perfect! We should get married here!"

They investigated and found out that others had the same idea. "But we managed to get the date we wanted, and as soon-to-be graduates, we were entitled to the alumni rate. It was a huge savings from other ceremony sites."

Tradition, Tradition

Tammie and Matt decided on a traditional church wedding. "There was some initial family discussion about which church. Our family is Methodist; Matt's is Presbyterian. In the end, maybe because my parents were paying, Matt's family told us we should get married in my family's church."

Because they wanted to show their appreciation for a peaceful resolution to what they had been afraid would be a tense situation, Tammie and Matt decided that they would look for a reception site that would honor his parents.

Help Us Celebrate!

JoEllen and Ben didn't find themselves agreeing

quickly on their wedding site. "We knew we wanted to have a big party, and it didn't seem quite right to have that in a church reception hall. Then, too, we aren't members of a church, so we didn't think we wanted to ask if we could get married in one and never go back."

Then JoEllen remembered a marina country club where she and Ben had had dinner one Sunday evening. "The sunset cast this lovely glow over the water, and we held hands, and it was such a special moment. I told Ben about what I'd remembered and how I thought it would be great to get married on the deck just as the sun was setting. His face lit up. 'Perfect,' he said. So we made the arrangements." The marina country club is pricey, so it's a good thing that JoEllen and Ben are planning within the luxurious wedding range!

Destination Weddings

What do you think about having your wedding when you are already at your honeymoon destination? Some couples are finding this a great choice. Destination weddings can take place in the United States or at a resort or hotel in an exotic locale—even a cruise ship. Sometimes couples feel that they are saving money by combining the sites. Others feel that although the expense can be high, the beauty of a ceremony and honeymoon in an exotic and romantic setting is worth the extra cash.

Is It Worth the Challenges? You Decide

There can be a number of challenges in planning a destination wedding. You have to deal with unfamiliar regulations regarding getting married, work with vendors you don't know, and have fewer guests at the wedding because of the expense—this final point may be seen as either a negative or a positive, depending on how you feel about having some family members at your wedding!

 FACT

Marriages of U.S. citizens in foreign countries are recognized legally in this country. Consult with officials in the country you want to be married in (see if they have a consulate in the United States) for requirements well ahead of the date you want to be married.

However, the negatives may be overwhelmed by the positives of being married in a destination you like enough to choose for your honeymoon. There's something very romantic about the idea. Savings can still be possible if you factor in all the things you won't need—including transportation, all those flowers for the church and reception (chances are, the destination is gorgeous and full of flowers), lots of wedding-party gifts, and other things.

Ask the Destination for Help

It's also possible to save money, time, and trouble by asking the destination if a wedding or event consultant is available to help you arrange a wedding. Be sure to ask if there is any fee for these services (most destinations are eager for your business and provide these services at no extra charge).

Questions to Ask

The best part of a destination wedding is using the location's natural elements—the beautiful natural setting of Hawaii, for instance, inspires a special mood for a wedding ceremony. What is it about your potential destination site that inspires you to say your vows there?

Ten important things to consider when planning a destination wedding are:

1. Can your family and wedding party travel to the site?
2. Who will pay for their airfare and accommodations?
3. What types of arrangements are available for on-site weddings?
4. Can you get an upgrade on your accommodations by having your wedding at the same site?
5. How many rooms can the site provide for your guests?
6. Will you be able to secure a special rate for accommodations? (Check with the airlines, too.)
7. When do you have to make a deposit and how much must it be?
8. Ask to see sample menus and photos of actual

weddings that have taken place at the destination.

9. Are there any special weather considerations? (Is it a prime location for hurricanes? Tropical storms?)

10. Is there a one-year anniversary return special for having a wedding there? (Some stateside and overseas hotels offer this to their guests who marry at their site.)

 ALERT!

Dozens of Web sites on destination weddings can be found on the Internet. You can find out about the most popular wedding destinations, check out some bargains, and even chat online with other couples who have chosen to have a destination wedding and are willing to share their experiences.

CHAPTER 4
The Reception Site

According to most people, and most wedding experts, the reception is the most costly part of the wedding budget. Couples enthusiastically plan a terrific party for their friends and family to celebrate their marriage. Then, suddenly, they're in over their heads and spending too much money!

The Big Day, Act II

Many people get caught up in the emotion and excitement of planning a wedding and start adding extras left and right. Whether it's people you decide to invite at the last minute, or little extra touches that you've realized you must have . . . suddenly, the figure that seemed like it might just work with some tweaking here and there is a distant memory. First, you add this expense, then those other expenses in other parts of your budget mushroom, and finally—*pow!*—there goes the budget.

 ALERT!

> If your guest list is getting out of hand, put the brakes on it, quick! Every extra guest, every extra thing you add, adds up to lots of money—fast—no matter what your budget.

It doesn't have to be that way. Take a deep breath and remember what's important here. It's your wedding day, not a day to give people the meal or the dance of their lifetime. It's about remembering what's important— having the people you care about and who care about you there to help you celebrate one of the most special days of your life.

When it really comes down to it, no one wants to see you bankrupt or stressed because of the wedding or the reception. Even if you have a luxurious budget, you still want to spend your money wisely.

Returning to That Quiz

Remember that quiz you and your fiancé took in Chapter 1? Let's return to it for a moment.

Where did the two of you envision having your reception? Was it at the church reception hall after the ceremony? At a hotel? At a beautiful park or historic area? At either of your parents' homes? Is there someplace that has become special to the two of you that would serve as "just the place" to celebrate your marriage?

Your Options Are Diverse

One option is to choose a civic or community center; there are many of these in most cities. One center, which has a museum-type gallery and a small stage with a piano, was the perfect site for a winter wedding. The bride and her bridesmaids turned the gallery into a fairy-tale setting of silk ficus topiary trees strung with twinkling lights and wrapped with tulle rented from a local florist.

 FACT

> The chamber of commerce, private estates, and historical societies often have buildings that are available for functions. Depending on the size of your wedding, consider one of these offbeat alternatives.

When the lights were dimmed and candles were set on the tables in rented candelabra, the gallery became a truly magical setting. The beautiful artwork on the walls just contributed to the elegance of the room, and a kitchen was close by for the caterer.

Other Great Reception Ideas

Country clubs, marinas, museums, private estates, or art centers are good reception sites. So are fellowship halls such as the V.F.W. You might also consider having the wedding at a church or other location and then hosting the reception at the home of one of your parents. Perhaps they have a lovely garden patio or a pool where a reception might be held.

One couple had their reception in the private lounge of the oceanside restaurant where they'd had their first date. The lounge was just big enough for the family and a half dozen wedding guests, and they had a great time.

 FACT

You might think you know your area, but chances are there are places you haven't even heard of that would make lovely wedding and reception sites. Check with your local chamber of commerce or research local or state Web sites, travel bureaus, and so on. The list of places and people eager to help you get married there will surprise you.

Several national television programs have filmed weddings and receptions that have taken place at Disney World in Orlando, Florida. Other theme parks and attractions have also played host to brides and grooms.

Location, Location, Location

Visit at least two places that *each* of you thinks would make a good reception location. Maybe you took the suggestion to "make it a date" when you looked for your ceremony site. Do it again, and look for that other important site. The idea is to stay flexible in your thinking and see what you come up with. Sometimes the planning for a wedding gets so intense, you just want to decide things, pay the money, and get it settled. Getting it settled, however, should not mean settling!

Church Reception Halls

Perhaps your fiancé likes the idea of having the reception in the hall attached to your church or synagogue. Nearly one out of four couples has the reception there, often because the bride or the groom, or both, are members of the church and it seems right to stay there after the ceremony. There's a sense of rightness to the place that makes you want to continue your celebration there.

There's no question about it—it's very convenient to have the reception at your place of worship. Guests can move easily into the next area while you have your wedding pictures taken, without getting into cars and driving over to a reception elsewhere. If you're in an area with bad weather in the winter, one location can be a real bonus.

 ESSENTIAL

Check with the church regarding its rules about using the hall, particularly about possible restrictions on serving alcoholic drinks, dancing, and so on. It may also have rules about what hours you may rent the hall, and how you may decorate it.

It's not likely that you'll experience problems with a church or synagogue in regards to broken promises, service problems, or any of the many challenges that can be associated with other reception sites. Because you already have an established relationship with the facility, you have a reduced risk of complications, conflicts, and potential crises. (That's not to say you shouldn't be just as diligent about setting expectations and getting the details in writing, both for your peace of mind and for that of whoever is responsible for the hall.)

Convenience, price break (over hotels and so on), and because it's an easy way to resolve several factors are all fine reasons to remain at your church or synagogue. Add to that the fact that most reception halls are well maintained and often decorated, and you have quite a plus. Whatever your motivation, you won't find others wondering why you wanted to hold the reception there.

It's an Important Day—Choose Carefully

Perhaps you've always wanted to have a reception someplace elegant like a hotel, not the church reception hall. Maybe a flower-filled garden setting seems perfect for your reception, or perhaps you know of a beautiful riverside park.

Whatever it is, set aside those few hours together and visit the locations—really look them over and talk about the vision each of you has for the reception. Think about what kind of celebration both you and your guests could have there.

Just like the site where you'll be married, you'll always remember the place where you celebrated your wedding, so make it a place that is truly special to you, whether your reception will be an event that is attended by a small group of friends and family, or a truly big gathering.

Open-Air Receptions

Amanda and Dustin talked about where they'd have their reception right after they decided to hold the wedding ceremony by the reflecting pool on the campus of their college.

"We looked at a few places, like the fancy reception rooms they have for functions for special guests on campus," Amanda said. "We also checked out some other places like meeting rooms at restaurants, and places like that."

ALERT!

Depending on your location and the season, an outdoor reception might be an option. If you decide on one, have a backup plan in case of bad weather.

Amanda and Dustin gave a little more thought to their vision. "We got to talking about how nice it was going to be to be outside in the sunshine, after all that time in classrooms, and we had that harpist . . . well, it just seemed natural to stay there and have a picnic with the two dozen or so people we invited."

Other Money-Saving Facilities

Tammie and Matt decided that the women's club that her mother is a member of was a perfect choice. Each year, the club's facility hosts many weddings for children of members, as well as others from the community.

"The catering would be a bit steeper than we planned, but still much less than a hotel reception," she said. "My dad offered to give us money to elope instead of having a wedding and reception! We think he was joking."

Actually, because her mother is a member, there was a discount for renting the facility. "We compared the prices for a luncheon reception and a sit-down dinner, and we saved by choosing the luncheon—a buffet, actually."

Private clubs such as women's clubs or fraternal clubs offer many benefits to their members and to the community. Such places can accommodate all kinds of events and usually have everything you'll need—the space, the furnishings, kitchen facilities, parking, and sometimes even security.

 QUESTION?

What kind of services or resources can a small club provide?
Often the person in charge of renting out a private club can also recommend caterers, florists, and musicians who have done a good job for other events held there. Coordinators often keep albums of events held there, which offer a variety of decorating ideas, too.

All about the Party

The wedding reception is where JoEllen and Ben are planning to spend the largest part of their wedding budget, so finding the perfect place was very important to them.

"We'll have the wedding outside, on a small pavilion overlooking the water, at the marina country club; then we'll move inside to a sit-down dinner and later, a dance," JoEllen explained. "My list of 'have-to-haves' is simple: We have to have a place that serves champagne and drinks, and has a dance floor and space for the jazz group we want."

Although they want to have a big party for their family and friends to celebrate their wedding, JoEllen and Ben also know they don't want it to go on too long. "We've both been to receptions that went on for so long that people had too much to drink, and it wasn't pleasant," said Ben. "So prearranging a time for things to be over before JoEllen and I leave for the airport for Hawaii is important."

What to Look For

Does the site incorporate the qualities that you want? Is it romantic enough? Cheerful enough? Will it accommodate the number of guests you'll invite? Is there access for every guest's needs?

Time Is Money

What time of day will you have your reception? The day of the week and the time of day will directly affect the cost of your reception. If you plan your reception for mid-afternoon, guests won't expect a big sit-down meal. If you serve champagne or other alcoholic beverages, will guests expect them for the duration of the reception, and how much will that cost?

No matter the budget you are using—modest, moderate, or luxurious (splurge)—you *can* control the spending by giving some thought to timing and scheduling during the early stages of your planning.

ESSENTIAL

> The time will affect the cost of your wedding—but it will also set the mood. People's expectations for a Saturday-night event are much different than they are for a Sunday-afternoon gathering.

Look It Over

If you have the opportunity, visit your prospective reception site, and pay attention to the details. Walk through the interior and note the table linens and silverware that are used, note how the wait staff takes care of patrons, and check out the restrooms and other amenities.

Most public places and businesses are in compliance with federal disability guidelines, but if you have anyone in your wedding party who would find it a difficult place to gain access to, you might rethink the site.

What about Food?

Some reception sites have their own caterer(s), whereas others don't provide any services at all. Find out whether the site will prepare the food or if you must make your own arrangements. Some places will let you bring in your own caterer, but will charge a fee for not using their services. Then again, do you want the responsibility of looking for a caterer, or do you prefer the convenience of an all-in-one package? Be sure you get information for a variety of scenarios as you do your research.

The answers to this kind of questioning can significantly affect your decision—and will certainly affect your budget. Be mindful of time, money, and energy—and your ultimate priorities—as you make your decision.

Ask Your Reception Site Coordinator

So you've finally made your choice for your reception site. Before you put down a deposit, there are some important questions you need to ask the coordinator:

1. What is the rental charge for the date and hours we want? (Also ask about rates for other dates and hours, in case you decide to change.)
2. How many hours does it include?
3. What is the seating capacity for the room/hall we're renting?
4. What is provided/included?
5. Is parking/valet service included?
6. What is the cancellation policy?
7. Is catering provided, or can/must we arrange it ourselves?
8. If we choose to arrange the catering ourselves, is there a fee attached? (An unpleasant "hidden fee" at some reception sites may be passed along to you by your caterer or by the facility.)

9. What about alcohol? May we bring our own, and if we do, is there a corkage or other fee? Can we arrange an open bar, and what are the rates for that?

10. If we'd like to bring a band/deejay/ensemble, is there a place for them to set up, and is there any charge for this?

11. Is there a cleanup fee, or is cleanup included in the price?

12. Can we rent other necessities such as tableware, linens, candleholders, and so on? What are the setup and/or cleanup fees associated with additional services?

QUESTION?

Are there little-known perks to using a hotel?
Some hotels offer the wedding couple a free night's stay on their first anniversary. Ask if they'll offer this to you. It's a nice way to celebrate your special day there, and save money, too!

Ask any of the coordinators you meet if they have any pictures of events that have been held at the reception site. And, as always, ask for references—and *use* them—to minimize the chance that you'll encounter problems. Many sites will also offer you a taste test of the food that you'll be served. If they don't, try to ask for it.

No Surprises!

JoEllen and Ben knew that they wouldn't need to ask for a taste of the food because they'd been to the marina country club for dinner. But when they made the formal arrangements, the club's coordinator still made sure they had a tour of the place and spent time reviewing the details, making sure they'd have the reception they wanted.

If you have other questions, now is the time to ask them, before you put down your deposit. (Remember, use a credit card in case you have problems later.)

The Deposit's Down—Now What?

The fun is just beginning! You have made two of the biggest decisions—and countless little ones, too. It's time to take a deep breath and relax a little. Just think of all the decisions you've made, all the investigating you've done, all the discussing and compromising you've gone through.

If you've brought it all in under budget so far, good for you! If not, then the rest of the book will be even more important in helping you have the wedding you want, within the budget you've set.

CHAPTER 5

Feed Them and They Will Come

After you have made plans about your reception site, consider what you want served at the reception. Reception food often becomes the subject of debate for wedding planners, but don't despair. You don't need to send your guests home hungry in order to stick to your budget. This chapter will show you how to pick the best food and beverages for your particular wedding reception.

How Much Can You Expect to Pay?

Reception food is usually calculated on a per-person basis. For instance, let's say you want to invite two hundred people for a sit-down dinner, and the least expensive meal you can get at your reception site is $30. Simple math quickly shows that this will cost you $6,000. But what if you don't have—or want—to spend that much on reception food? You have two options: You can either keep the number of guests to a minimum, or you can avoid a sit-down dinner and save on the per-person fee.

 FACT

> Weddings and receptions that begin at midday or later tend to be more popular and better attended. That means that more of your invited guests will show up; you need to take that into consideration for your headcount.

Alternatives to a Sit-Down Dinner

First, decide what time of the day you want to get married. That will dictate the time of the reception. In basic terms, the earlier in the day you get married, the less expensive the meal choices will be. Get married at sunrise, and you can have a wedding breakfast or brunch.

Luncheon or tea menus cost a bit more, but again, they're less expensive than a sit-down dinner. And dinnertime receptions pose another problem—whether you should serve alcoholic beverages, and, if so, whether they should be "on the house" or sold at a cash bar. (An unlimited, or open, bar will hike up your reception costs to the extreme.)

Money-Saving Menus

Some suggestions for a simple breakfast/brunch menu in the modest budget category might be scrambled eggs, a breakfast meat popular in your region (such as bacon or sausage), potatoes, fruit, sweet rolls, coffee, tea, and juice. This same general menu could be adapted to the moderate budget by offering omelets with several fillings, two breakfast meats, home fries or grits (again, depending on regional tastes), an assortment of breakfast pastries, coffee, tea, hot chocolate, and several juices.

 ESSENTIAL

A luxurious wedding breakfast/brunch would include eggs Benedict or a similar egg specialty, crêpes or Belgian waffles, spiral-sliced ham or shrimp cocktail, fruit compote, flavored coffees or cappuccinos, teas, several juice selections, and mimosas (champagne cocktails made with orange juice).

Try to select a simple menu using foods in season. Remember: "Simple" doesn't mean mediocre—you need to think "uncomplicated." Although you can now get almost any kind of food in any season by importing it, those costs can add up. And food grown fairly locally and in season will be freshest—just think how good some spring vegetables such as asparagus taste. Plan an in-season menu and, when possible, be ready to substitute if conditions change or your food supplier can offer a better choice or price.

So, let's say you've decided on an early wedding. Don't think it needs to be a sit-down occasion. If you want to save money, you can offer a table set with breakfast pastries, coffee, tea, and juices if you wish. If you are using a moderate budget, you could feature a buffet table with your menu choices. If you want to save on a sit-down dinner (regardless of your budget), don't order elaborate sauces or complicated prepared dishes. Consider how these dishes and the staff needed to serve them will add to the cost.

Avoid a Meal Altogether

Some couples are skipping wedding meals by scheduling their reception at nonmeal times such as mid-afternoon or after dinner, and indicating that they will feature an hors d'oeuvres selection or a dessert buffet and appropriate beverages. Either of these can be a very classy option.

Catering Service

If you are having your reception at a hotel or a restaurant, you'll have to use their services (and one of your reasons for choosing that location may in fact be because you want to serve their food). If your reception is at a location that does not have food service and you don't want to prepare the food yourself, then you will need a caterer.

 QUESTION?

How can you find an off-site caterer if you've never used one before?
Get a list of caterers from your reception site or from other vendors such as your wedding coordinator or florist. If there is a culinary school or an educational institution in your area that provides catering services, you might want to try them, too.

Ask Questions

Don't be intimidated if you've never dealt with a caterer before. Here are some questions to ask to make sure you get what you want for what you want to spend:

1. What can you offer us for our budget?
2. What about substitutions for special diets?
3. Will we need to provide our own dishes, silverware, napkins, and so on? (Make sure the quality of all

the utensils is appropriate for the reception you're planning—ask to see samples.)

4. How many servers will there be, and will they do cleanup?
5. Is there a charge to cut the cake? Serve it?
6. What is the deposit schedule? When do you need a final count?

Some reception sites will charge the caterer a fee, and that fee will be added to your bill. Ask both the site and the caterer about their policies regarding these types of charges.

Cruise Those Menus

Regardless of who provides the food, you can save a lot of money by asking a lot of questions and carefully looking over menus so that you will get the most for your budgeted dollars. If either the on-site or the private caterers tend to feature mostly very gourmet entrées, you could ask if you can substitute something less expensive.

Being careful with your dollars doesn't have to mean you serve another institutional chicken dinner. Think creatively—certain herbs, spices, and other fairly simple touches can transform the bird into something quite elegant but not as expensive as *coq au vin.* Even if you want to splurge and have prime rib, not all guests eat beef these days, so you'll want to provide something different for them anyway. Thinking outside the box with your entrée choices can mean a delicious meal for less money.

JoEllen and Ben would save some money by having both their ceremony and reception at the club, so they could afford to order pricier dishes, but they have kept their fancy reception menu of island favorites relatively simple—seafood salad, fresh lobster, stir-fried vegetables, and ambrosia served in pineapple shells.

After they picked the menu, they were told that they could also save by allowing the chef to substitute different seafood and fruit (with their permission) if he hears of a better price or better in-season quality.

 ALERT!

Don't avoid the tastings! Make an appointment with a caterer to taste some samples of your menu choices. Ask to see photos of their work, too. Be sure to ask for references and *call them!* And always, *always,* get everything in writing to prevent misunderstandings or inadequate amounts.

How to Avoid Catering Service

You're not really going to have that reception without Aunt Fran's special antipasto platter, are you? Or Grandma Joanna's special-occasion champagne punch? No, really?

Family has always been an extremely important part of wedding days and is becoming even more important today. Perhaps some members of your family would like to get more involved in your wedding, and food preparation is a perfect opportunity.

Do You Have Family Favorites?

Even if you want to have your reception at a fancy hotel, or an off-site caterer is preparing the food, there may still be some foods and beverages that you just can't imagine being fixed by someone other than a particular family member or friend.

Check to make sure that you can bring those special food and beverage items to your reception site so they're not wasted or that feelings aren't hurt. There should be enough of whatever is being brought for most of your guests to have a taste, and the food or beverage should be stored at the proper temperature so that there are no food poisoning issues to ruin the day.

Families Made Their Day

Because Amanda and Dustin are planning to have a casual wedding done on a very modest budget, they don't want to spend money on an elaborate meal. Even though their college cafeteria occasionally does provide catering services, this option wasn't even discussed.

Amanda's aunt has enjoyed preparing elegant box lunches for her garden and community clubs for years, and when she suggested it to her niece, Amanda jumped at the idea. "It seems perfect to have this kind of food at our outdoor wedding!" Her aunt refused to take any money for the supplies from Amanda, insisting that this would be her wedding present. It was agreed that Amanda's aunt would prepare fancy tea sandwiches, little containers of her famous pasta and potato salads, and crudités, tucked into fancy little white boxes, tied with yellow ribbon, and decorated with sprigs of silk daisies. Iced tea and lemonade would be served as well.

Champagne and Other Libations

What beverages will you serve at your reception? Time of day plays an important part in determining what your best options are. Bottles of champagne or other alcoholic beverages aren't freely passed around at a morning wedding reception. A mimosa or maybe a Bloody Mary could be offered at a brunch, but there would be a limit on the amount because of the hour. At luncheons and mid-afternoon weddings, champagne punch and champagne toasts are appropriate. Again, the time of day dictates that the amount be controlled. During late afternoon or evening weddings, alcoholic beverages can get expensive if they are not controlled.

Don't Let the Dollars Fizz Away

Alcohol can be a huge expense at a reception. Do you want to have a champagne toast? You'll need to check on the alcohol policy at your reception site so you can plan better. Some church reception halls, fraternal halls, and community centers don't permit alcohol at all; many hotels and restaurants want you to buy from them. Is there a charge for corkage or a special bar and bartender arrangement in place?

Get in writing exactly what you'll be charged for, and make certain the contract includes a stipulation that you'll be consulted if the drink consumption looks as though it will exceed the predetermined dollar amount. A "no-host" or cash bar—one that charges your guests for their drinks—is usually not considered appropriate.

 ESSENTIAL

> If you are providing the alcoholic beverages, be sure your vendor will allow you to return unopened bottles. If you're not a wine expert—and most of us are not!—get a friend or knowledgeable person to guide you in selecting a good vintage with a reasonable price.

Beverages on Different Budgets

Amanda and Dustin can't have alcohol at their college site, so they'll be toasted with sparkling white grape juice in elegant glasses.

Tammie and Matt plan on having one champagne toast; their Grandma Joanna's special champagne punch will be served for the remainder of the ceremony. "We couldn't imagine a wedding reception or celebration that didn't involve the punch. What's a nice bonus is how it's not only delicious; it's a money saver over having straight champagne." The punch will be served in an antique punch bowl that's been in the family for years.

JoEllen and Ben plan on having champagne and mixed drinks at their reception, but to prevent overimbibing, they will have a cutoff limit established with their bartender, nonalcoholic drinks for designated drivers and teetotalers, and an arrangement with a taxi company to take home guests who try to leave too merry to drive.

Whether you serve spiked or nonalcoholic punch, consider renting a punch fountain. These are generally available at most hotels and from caterers. Although they are relatively inexpensive, they can add a nice touch to your reception.

The Perfect Wedding Cake

How much do you want to budget for your cake? If you have a modest or moderate budget and the cake is not one of the most important elements of your day, something simple like a two- or three-layer cake iced simply and topped with some flowers would be the least expensive choice.

However, if the cake is a high-priority item for you, consider ordering something more elaborate, such as a multi-layered cake with special decorations, or one made of many layers of various flavors of cheesecake. Many other choices exist, including cakes filled with fruit, mousse, or fillings made of liqueurs like Amaretto and Grand Marnier. Frostings can be butter cream, Bavarian cream, whipped cream, or fondant.

ALERT!

First, decide what flavor of cake you like. If you find that you like vanilla and he likes chocolate, you can do both—it's your cake! With all the choices today, you don't have to settle for a white cake with white frosting and the same old stiff sugar flower decorations. The options are endless.

What Are Your Needs?

When deciding on a cake, consider your needs. How many guests have you invited? Do you want to save the top layer of your cake, to freeze and enjoy on your first anniversary? Will you want a groom's cake as well? Your baker will need to know the answers to these questions in order to tell you how big a cake you'll need. The size and complexity of the cake as well as where and when it needs to be delivered will determine the price.

Top It Off

A cake could be decorated with icing patterns that look like lace or fresh roses, and be placed on an antique porcelain cake stand. A couple was featured on television recently with a cake that had a castle as its topper—and the couple was delighted to tell the viewers that they had saved by borrowing the topper from a prop company. A cake for a western wedding might feature a cowboy and his bride cake topper, even a whimsical cow couple atop a cake decorated with cow spots! A cake decorated with sugar seashells would be wonderful for a beach wedding or one held near the ocean.

Personalize your cake with something that reflects your interests, such as your career or hobbies or your military experience. Do the two of you like to sky dive or scuba dive? You might want a cake topper to really show off this interest. Individuals who make custom cake toppers can make something special that may become a treasured family heirloom. Given a picture or detailed description of a specialty cake, local bakers might be able to duplicate what you have in mind for less expense.

 FACT

When the estates of the Duke and Duchess of Windsor were sold at auction recently, a beribboned box inscribed "A piece of our wedding cake" sold for $26,000 in a very spirited bidding contest! "It's history," said an auction attendee. "He gave up being king of England for his bride."

Seasonal Cakes

One bride who planned a Christmas wedding found a beautiful blown-glass gazebo ornament with a couple embracing within it. The price was right—under $20. A friend baked a simple round three-layer cake and covered it with a simple white icing; then, she placed red silk poinsettias, holly, and evergreen around the base. The friend hot-glued the bottom of the ornament to a six-inch round mirror and placed it atop the cake. When the light hit the topper, the sparkle was fantastic. It was a bargain, but no one knew.

A similar look could be translated to another season very easily by using different colored flowers. Spring or summer flowers could be placed at the base; autumn-colored leaves and seasonal fruit would be appropriate for fall.

Finding the Right Baker

What is the situation with bakers where you live? Do you live in a bigger city where there are not only many bakeries but also many different types, or do you live in a small town where only one or two bakeries exist—or maybe there is only a small bakery inside a grocery store? Is there a pastry chef at your reception site who will bake the cake? (Some sites insist on your ordering your cake from them.) Will you order a cake from a baker who advertises on the Internet? Do you have a family member or friend who wants to bake your cake? There are so many choices—think of them as opportunities to save!

Finding a Special Baker

Once again, you'll save your money by going with bakers you've found through references from family and friends, or acquaintances who have been married recently or attended a wedding. Choosing a baker from out of the phone book—with whom you are unfamiliar—can be chancy.

Questions to ask your baker:

1. Do you have pictures of cakes you've made for other weddings?
2. If we want something different, can you do a customized cake for me?
3. If we need a cake for a certain number of guests, how much will that cost? (Prices can range from $1 a slice up to $10—or more—depending on your area and how fancy a cake you want.)
4. Will you deliver the cake to our reception site? Is there a delivery charge? A setup charge? (You don't want the unpleasant surprise of an unassembled cake arriving and the delivery person disappearing.)
5. How far ahead must we order the cake? How much of a deposit must we put down?

 ESSENTIAL

Some unique ways to save on your wedding cake include having fake layers to add height but not dollars (and wasted cake), having cakes on pedestals of varying heights instead of one big stacked cake, and decorating with flowers instead of lots of fancy frosting details and/or a cake topper.

Getting the Most for Your Money

Of course, getting everything in writing will ensure that the cake you pay for is the same one that is delivered to your wedding. Don't order a bigger cake than you need—if you're serving desserts or have chosen to have a groom's cake, you won't need as many slices.

Having a taste of several cakes while you're at your bakery might make a big difference in how much you'll spend. If the baker has a really good tasting yellow cake, for instance, you might choose not to spend so much on a carrot cake or cheesecake and can save the dollars for something else.

 ALERT!

Be sure that the cake won't be delivered too early, possibly getting ruined by sitting in a location that is too warm, or jostled by people setting up the reception site. If it's an outdoor location, is there protection for the cake from insects?

When a Cake's Not a Cake

One clever bride recently chose to have elegant flower-trimmed cupcakes placed on a big-tiered pedestal stand. This way each guest could have an individual serving and she saved on the price of a big cake. The children at the wedding weren't the only ones who were delighted. The cupcakes were very moist because they were baked in their paper cups, and the icing touches atop them were as elegant as any full-size cake.

Some couples save by having a fancy cake for the wedding photos and then serving slices of sheet cake, cut in the kitchen where the guests can't see. Another way to save is to have cake layers of different sizes placed on acrylic stands and grouped, with the largest at the center front of the table.

Whatever kind of cake you choose, it should have an honored place at the reception with its own table (less apt to be jostled than at the head table!) and decorations.

CATERER WORKSHEET

ITEM	DESCRIPTION	COST
appetizers		
entrées		
dessert		
other food		
beverages		
champagne		
wine		
liquor		
equipment		
tent		
chairs		
tables		
linens		
dinnerware		
flatware		
glassware		
serving pieces		
service		
servers		
bartenders		
valet parking		
attendants		
coat checkers		
overtime cost		
other		

TOTAL:

CHAPTER 6
The Clothes That Make the Wedding

ow it's time to talk about the bride's dress—one of the bigger expenses of your wedding budget! Some budget guides will advise you to spend a certain percentage or a "piece of the pie" and use a pie chart to demonstrate this concept of the clothing portion of the wedding budget. Oh, please!

What Will You Wear?

Don't start your search with the price tag. It's a much better idea to start looking for what will be appropriate for the location you've chosen for your ceremony. Find out where or how you can find the attire that will work best, and then, if need be, modify your choices to fit your budget.

Making a Budget for Your Dress

What is the budget you've chosen for your dress? Remember that you do not have to be bound by a smaller budget for your dress if it is one of your "priority" items for the wedding. Perhaps you want to spend more to get what you want and cut down on expenses elsewhere. This is perfectly understandable. It's an important day for you, and you want to look gorgeous. After all, you'll be looking at those wedding pictures for a long, long time.

Picture Your Dress

Do you have a picture of the kind of dress you want in your head? Does it suit the location you've chosen? A big, formal dress with a sweeping train won't work if you have to walk down a grassy path outdoors for your ceremony—well, not unless you don't mind grass stains! A dress with long sleeves for a summertime outdoors wedding won't work either. We've all heard the horror stories about brides passing out from the heat as they stand at the altar. Grooms are nervous enough. They don't need to see you fainting right in front of them!

FACT

> A great way to save is to buy a sleeveless gown
> to wear in any season. Shop around for some
> end-of-summer deals. If you're getting married
> in the winter or in a cold location, add a lace or
> velvet jacket or wrap. These can be discarded if
> you get too warm dancing!

Do you want a long gown or a short one? Simple or elaborate? You can get most any kind of gown for any kind of budget, depending on how willing you are to compromise. Want an elaborate gown for a little money? Consider buying a previously used gown, or a designer sample. Do you favor a simple design but love the expensive beadwork on a more expensive gown (maybe a designer's)? Consider buying the beads from a fabric store and sewing them on yourself to save money—it's really easy!

Start your gown search by looking through bridal magazines. Clip pictures of the looks you like for the season you'll be married in. Also look through any photos you can find of weddings that have taken place in the location you've chosen.

Style Guides

Countless bride magazine sites will help you decide on the dress style you prefer so you'll know what you want when you're ready to go shopping. And doing your homework can be great if you don't know how to use the jargon necessary to ask for what you want. Who needs to feel uneducated about what that neckline or sleeve style is called?

Knowing the types of necklines and other features and whether they look good on you will also save you time and money in the bridal stores. When you speak the same language, you and the bridal consultant or saleswoman can work together to find what you want. You also won't be apt to get so overtired and stressed trying to find the right dress that you get talked into something more expensive than you want, or a style that you're not happy with.

Do a topic search on your favorite search engine, and you'll be guaranteed hundreds of sites where you can shop for bridal apparel—or just great ideas that will help you when you shop in a store in your area.

 ESSENTIAL

Save yourself time and money by going online and checking out ✑ *www.weddingchannel.com*. One of the features of this site allows you to create a virtual model with your body shape, height, hair color, and similar facial structure. "Try on" various gown and veil styles, and then print them out for future reference.

As mentioned previously, the first place to start is with the major bride magazines, which all have very detailed Web sites that have many, many suggestions about wedding dresses as well as every other aspect of a wedding.

Looking for Bargains

Consignment shops are great places to find bargains. Sometimes brides buy a gown, then change their wedding date, and the gown is no longer appropriate for the new season. There you have it—a never-worn gown at reduced price!

 FACT

If you are planning a moderate or luxurious (splurge) wedding, check out *www.kathryn andalexandra.com*. Costume designers for films, Kathryn and Alexandra make custom gowns and specialize in period wedding dresses. The prices are often competitive with the upper-range designer dresses, which aren't as rare.

Going Vintage

Although some gowns in a vintage shop can be pricey, you can still find bargains. Consider this option especially if you are getting married in a historical type of setting, such as a local mansion. A vintage dress will complement the mood of your ceremony site and make you feel elegant. Some of the gowns in the 1920s and 1930s inspired the slinky styles fashionable today and often don't cost much. Finish off the look with some vintage accessories, like a long string of pearls or glass beads, a beaded purse, or a period hat.

Vintage clothing is a marvelous touch for weddings of all budgets, depending on the quality and age of the garments. One caution, though—larger sizes are harder to find in vintage clothing.

Check the Classifieds

It's possible to find a lovely dress and stay within a budget by checking out the classified ads in the newspaper. One bride found a beautiful gown by visiting dry-cleaning stores in her area. Think again about that attitude toward secondhand goods. Today, they offer great opportunities to get something much better than brand-new (and not always as well constructed) for less money.

Look in Your Mother's Closet

For real savings and a glimpse of cherished memories, look in your mother's closet. Yes, really! For sentimental reasons, many brides wear the gowns their mothers, grandmothers, or other female relatives wore. And family gowns are also great money savers!

If the gowns are still around and in good shape, you can have them professionally cleaned and altered. Occasionally the more delicate headpieces don't survive storage, but either you or a seamstress can easily replicate them with the aid of pictures.

QUESTION?

What if my mother's gown is not available any more?
Duplicate it by finding a pattern, material, and a seamstress to stitch up a copy for you. No one will know that it's not the same gown unless you tell them!

Even Better: Free!

Do you have a friend or relative who will loan you a dress? Nothing's better than free—well, except for what you pay to have it cleaned before you return it!

Or what about sharing? Two sisters shared a gown for their weddings that were a few months apart. They loved the idea because they'd always been very close emotionally and this made for a special memory. Besides the money savings, this way they were able to have something a little better quality and still save dollars. Fortunately they were close in size and needed to do only minor alterations.

Think of It as a Lease

Renting a dress is also an option. Think of it as leasing your dream dress and not paying all that money for one use. One bride who was having a luxurious wedding decided to save money by renting her dress. "No one knew," she said afterward. "Since the rest of the wedding was so nice, it wasn't as if anyone suspected. We were able to spend the money on having a nicer reception."

How to Shop

Whether you use eBay or a lesser-known auction site, it's important to be a smart consumer. Be honest with yourself about sizes and preferences, too. Don't buy a dress that will need lots of alterations, because that will eat away at whatever you've saved by purchasing your dress at auction.

 FACT

> eBay is full of wedding styles at bargain prices, offered by individuals as well as bridal stores. How about tiaras under $10, gowns for $25, a $4,000 Vera Wang worn just once for $1,500? Grooms and the rest of the wedding party can find great deals there, too!

Outlets Are In

Bridal outlets are springing up in more and more cities these days. While you might not choose the $99 dress bargains they advertise, you will see a large selection of dresses. Be careful of the pressure to buy wherever you visit, but most particularly in the huge warehouses and smaller specialty shops where over-head is high.

If you have a lot of time to plan for your wedding, as much as a year, it's possible to shop at the end of the season for a dress for the following year. Also, think about having a dress made if you or someone you trust knows a seamstress who's experienced at sewing such gowns.

Most importantly, be creative—keep your mind open to the options of what's possible. Check out department stores, especially the formalwear sections, and catalogs. That simple, floor-length cocktail sheath could be a perfect wedding dress; all you need to do is add a few decorative touches.

Three Choices

You may have a vision of the dress you want, but remember that the time, place, and formality of an individual wedding will determine what kind of gown you need. The appropriateness of the gown for the setting of your ceremony is as important to its overall effect as how it actually looks on you.

A Dress for a Country Club Wedding

"I didn't want something as fussy and formal as if I were getting married in a church," JoEllen said. "And, of course, it had to be elegant and easy to dance in." She chose a short ivory candlelight dress and added a chiffon stole that would flutter in the breeze off the water as she and Ben walked along the wooden deck of the marina country club.

A Dress for a Traditional Church Wedding

Opting for the traditional, Tammie found a dress with a cathedral-length train but found it in an unorthodox source—a wedding finery rental store. "I never thought I'd do this," she confided. "But when I realized I could get something so special for a fraction of the cost, I did it." The rental cost Tammie just $275, instead of the $1,200 she had budgeted.

Super Savings on a Small Wedding

Amanda had a hectic last semester at college and couldn't spare a lot of time to look around for her dress. "I studied the pictures of summer weddings held outdoors and realized that those dresses wouldn't work in my setting—or my budget! So I started looking for a simpler kind of dress, with a tea-length hem that wouldn't brush the grass—something that would carry out my fresh, outdoor theme. There was a dress online that looked perfect for a summer wedding. I bid on it and got it for $75!"

But something was missing. "I'd been looking at the bride magazines and saw that hats were becoming popular again," Amanda said, "so I splurged on a beautiful wide-brimmed hat and trimmed it with some silk daisies to match the real ones I'd be carrying in my bouquet. I sewed a few on the hem of the dress, and I had a beautiful outfit."

ALERT!

This point can't be stressed enough: Wherever you shop, remember to be a wise consumer and use that credit card. It will give you more leverage if the order isn't what you expected.

Remember that alterations can add quite a bit to the price of your purchased gown—especially if you're like many brides who lose weight and have multiple fittings and alterations. Be sure to get a written estimate of the cost and try not to go through drastic size changes. After all, that's not good for your health, and you have enough stress in your life now, anyway, right?

Then Again, Maybe You'll Splurge

One friend was determined to help her daughter find a wedding dress that fit their budget. They had saved on everything else and were feeling pretty good about their winning streak!

As she recounts, "My daughter tried on the first one, and as she came out of the dressing room, I saw a young man who was there looking at dresses with a young woman. I don't know if she was his fiancée or friend, but anyway, he shook her arm to get her attention and said, 'Oh, wow, look at her!' Now, the other young woman wasn't real happy at that remark at first, but she looked at my daughter and you could see she thought it made Sarah a beautiful bride.

"The dress was twice the budget we wanted to spend. I could tell Sarah thought this was 'The Dress,' you know, the one that they say you'll just know is *It*. She said that she could be happy with the dress that was more in our budget, but I just couldn't let her. We decided we'd find some way to save in other places." And they did.

Find Other Places to Save

"There was a headpiece to match the dress, and the price was outrageous," agreed Sarah. "It just bothered me to see what they wanted for a simple cloth scrunchy-looking thing that wrapped around my topknot. You know, a ponytail holder? I made a satin one to match my gown and attached a fingertip-length veil to it, and no one was the wiser. I spent next to nothing for the small amount of satin and the tulle for the veil."

 FACT

If you are even reasonably good with a needle or a glue gun, you can put together a headpiece that won't cost as much as those ready-made ones. Visit the bridal section at your local fabric or craft store. You'll be amazed at the variety and price of really top-quality items that will go together easily.

Wedding Gown Accessories

Once you have picked your gown, you will also need to consider matching shoes and jewelry, as well as other accessories—for example, a hat, a shawl, or a veil.

Shoes for Walking down the Aisle

Save the money you might be tempted to spend on overly decorated shoes that you'll wear just once—unless they're a high-priority item for you. Also remember that you don't have to get expensive dyeable shoes that you probably won't wear again. Check out the shoes you want to wear for comfort, and don't think they have to be high heels. There are many adorable styles that have low or flat heels, which are especially necessary for outdoor weddings!

You are certainly not limited to bridal shops for your shoe shopping. Begin your search at discount stores and all the places you go to look for bargains for everyday and dress shoes, rather than limiting yourself to just the bridal shops. Many brides wear shoes that are not those expensive satin ones the saleswoman may try to convince you are absolutely necessary.

Make sure you pick out a pair of shoes that you find comfortable—you're going to be on your feet a lot on your wedding day! And remember that the same is true for your attendants—don't force your bridesmaids to hobble down the aisle in shoes they might not feel at ease in.

Jewels for a Price

If you've been given a necklace by your fiancé or parents, you already have the special jewelry you want to wear for the wedding. If you don't have something that seems ideal, a simple strand of pearls or a chain with a drop pearl is an elegant and risk-free option. You'll find items like these for any budget in the costume jewelry sections of department stores and other shops. If you usually prefer jewelry in a different style, don't spend the money for genuine pearls you may not wear very often.

 ESSENTIAL

Take a look at museum gift shop catalogs that feature reproductions of exquisite, work-of-art jewelry for reasonable prices. You can make an inexpensive selection that will give you a megabucks look.

Now for the Groom

Who's looked at as much as the bride on the wedding day? Why, the groom, of course! And while he may be the handsomest man on the planet, some of the styles in the men's formalwear shop just don't cut it, do they? Does a man who looks great in casual wear like khakis and golf shirts just look uncomfortable in a cutaway? Or is he looking forward to putting on that cutaway?

What's interesting is that a man who normally exercises a lot of thought about his clothing will walk in and pick out just any old tux, as if they all look alike. In fact, there are all types of styles that flatter different body shapes. If the groom doesn't want you to go with him, perhaps his best man and his attendants can do so. As one men's formalwear Web site warns, you don't want your fiancé to walk out of the store with a polyester bell-bottom set from the 1970s.

Check Bridal Magazines for Him, Too

Glance through the bridal magazines to get a sense of what type of formalwear is appropriate for the type of wedding you're having, and then consult with your local tuxedo rental store. The biggest designers for men are Ralph Lauren, Tommy Hilfiger, Perry Ellis, and FUBU. Tuxes made by these designers are also available for sale.

The rules of what is worn at what time of the day or with what type of wedding are gone. Just like women, men are refusing to be ruled by the fashion tyrants. A tux is not even necessary—a simple, good suit in black or dark gray—even brown for summer—is appropriate for many weddings these days. Perhaps you're having a western wedding. Then you might want to go with a Texas formal style—tux jackets with new jeans and a Stetson.

As with rentals of other items for your wedding, it's important to place your order early. No one wants to find himself competing for a tux with the local high school prom-goers.

FACT

Generally, all the men in the wedding party order their formalwear from the same store to make certain that their look is consistent. Some stores will also offer a discount package such as a special rate for the groom's tux rental if he has a large number of attendants.

Virtual Shopping

Sit down with your fiancé and take a look at some of the Web sites that feature tuxedo rental stores. Good ones to check out are *www.afterhours.com* and *www.marryingman.com* (which flashes a reminder of how many days until The Big Day and encourages grooms to "Do It Now"—order the tux, that is!). You can look through the sites together and see what styles and colors would be appropriate for the kind of wedding you're planning.

Hairstyles and Makeup

Everyone has seen the bride who decides to use her wedding to try out a new look that just isn't her—whether it's a new hairstyle and makeup, or just too much of it. Ask your stylist to arrange a good time to get your haircut or body perm or hair color so that it looks its best for your wedding. You don't want any unpleasant surprises on your wedding day! If your hair "wilts" or turns frizzy on a damp day, discuss a backup plan for a different style.

Always take your veil, flowers, or whatever headpiece you're using with you. It's also a good idea to bring a Polaroid of your wedding dress so that you can both agree on a look that suits you best before the Big Day.

Think about consulting with a makeup expert at a counter in an upscale department store for advice on what colors and types of makeup to wear for different times of the day or season. You'll get some free advice on what looks good—just be careful not to go overboard and buy the expensive makeup that you won't use again!

 ALERT!

The groom should also be careful not to let his barber get carried away with the scissors and give him a cut that's too short just before the wedding. One bride confided that she never knew her new husband had such big ears— they were revealed when he got his new haircut, a few days before the wedding!

CHAPTER 7
Words for Inviting; Flowers to Delight In

So you're getting ready to spread the good news. The time has come to think about the invitations and the message you want to send to your honored guests. And as for flowers for your bouquet and decorating . . . enjoy the process of finding the perfect flowers for the perfect price.

Sending out the Announcements

Do you want a unique way to announce your engagement or invite friends and family to your wedding? Maybe. Maybe not. In either case, you need to realize that you don't have to be content with the one or two books of invitation samples offered by a bored teenaged clerk at the local stationery store.

Whether you live in a big city or a small town, you don't want every aspect of your wedding to take a lot of money and time. Now that you've decided on a time, date, and location for your wedding, planning your invitations and finally seeing the details in print gives you a wonderful feeling of "it's really going to happen," doesn't it?

Consider Your Options

The options that make your invitations fancier—such as engraving versus print, enclosures, and so on—affect more than the price of the invitations; they also increase the cost of the postage required to mail the invitations. If you are planning an extensive guest list, postage will add to what you need to account for in your budget.

 ALERT!

When you add up save-the-date notices and information, invitations, and response cards (not to mention thank-you notes!), postage will be a significant expense. Be sure that it's included in your budget.

Perhaps you're having a modest wedding with a small guest list and don't require hundreds of fancy invitations. Still, you want something special to announce your event. A larger moderate or luxurious budget might have room for more elaborate invitations, but you get to decide if you want to stay conservative or if you want to send a message that you are hosting a more elaborate wedding. The latter weddings, which will likely have significant budgets for receptions, should include a more detailed RSVP, to better plan catering expenses and any other necessary accommodations.

What's Your Invitation Budget?

How much have you budgeted for invitations? Are you planning a modest, moderate, or luxurious wedding? Obviously, your overall budget will dictate the amount you spend on invitations. If you're on a modest budget, you don't want to spend a large amount of money on invitations and then not have enough to budget for the kind of flowers or wedding cake you want.

Know Your Quantity

Be mindful of your budget when ordering the number of invitations, too. It's best to order an additional two dozen invitations in case you suddenly remember guests you should have invited. You may also want to give an extra invitation to your parents or members of your wedding party to include in photo or memory books.

Extra invitations and envelopes are helpful if there's a mistake in addressing them or some are returned for an incorrect address and you need to resend them. No one wants to have to go back to the printer with a small order and pay for express service or express mail.

 QUESTION?

What can you do with extra invitations?
Use your extra invitations to create gifts for your wedding party. Cut out pictures of you with your friends in the wedding party, paste them around the invitations, frame the collages, and present them to your bridesmaids and groomsmen.

A nice touch is to get a small album for the bride and groom's families and paste the invitation to the cover, hot-glue some decorations around it, and fill the inside with some photos of the wedding.

Invite the Internet In

It's great if you have a good stationery supplier in your town or city. And you'll be even better off if you have the time to sit and look through the books of samples. However, you have a great time and money saver in the Internet—it offers a whole world of styles, prices, and creative touches to suit any budget. Just type "wedding invitations" into your favorite search engine, and hundreds of sites will appear, many of which offer the same name brands carried by the best stationery stores. Prices can be anywhere from 15 to 30 percent lower than your local source's, but make sure you consider the shipping costs of dealing with an online stationery service.

If you're unsure of what you want, some sites such as *www.weddingdesignonline.com* offer you the opportunity to design your invitation and see how it will look. Free catalogs and samples are available, and many companies offer to send you a proof (that is, a sample) to make sure you're totally happy before you complete your order.

Express Yourself

So, you want your invitation to be different from everyone else's, but you also don't want to spend a lot of money. Stay with the least expensive cardstock and printing options, and then add your own unique features with a special or customized sealing stamp or ribbon that you can attach yourself.

You can always make your own wedding invitations: Buy kits at office supply or stationery stores to design them at home. All you need is a little time and a good printer. Perhaps you or your fiancé would really enjoy making your own invitations that incorporate your own special touch.

Special Touches

One bride and groom who were having a medieval wedding printed an 8½-by-11-inch piece of ivory paper, then rolled it and tied it with a ribbon—voilà, a scroll invitation! (This type of invitation cost a little more to mail because it needed mailing tubes, but the couple felt the extra expense was worth it.)

Another bride, getting married in a Victorian mansion, wanted more elaborate invitations but still didn't want to spend a lot. She chose rose-colored paper, a fancy font, and glued pressed flowers and lace medallions on the invitations.

 ALERT!

Watch out—the wedding invitation people are just waiting for you to be so enthused that you end up ordering hundreds of dollars' worth of their merchandise, including any combination of invitations with fancy ribbons and printing, foil papers, pressed flowers—the list is positively endless. Before you agree to everything, ask yourself, do you really need all that?

Another couple invited their guests to a western-style wedding with a chambray blue invitation that sported a rope border encircling the text. As you are deciding on your personal style, try to find one that conveys the tone of your wedding without adding significant expense.

ESSENTIAL

If you want to help your guests plan ahead, follow this example: Some couples are choosing to send out a save-the-date card, asking their guests to mark the date on a calendar. This way, couples have a little more time to plan the final details before sending invitations.

What about Our Three Couples?

After looking at several stationery stores and Internet sites, Amanda and Dustin thought about designing their own invitations but realized that they didn't really have enough time to do that. However, that initial look at invitations reminded them that a friend of theirs was a recent computer graphics graduate who often did freelance work for local businesses to help pay his tuition.

The friend is working with them on a simple design featuring Amanda's theme of a daisy wedding. A local office supply store will do the printing for a very reasonable price.

Tammie and Matt wanted invitations to suit their traditional wedding, with reception cards and special touches like wax seals on the outside of the envelope. They opted for a local stationer and were willing to pay a little extra for the invitations, feeling that they set the tone for the more formal nature of their wedding.

FACT

> Some couples are including their e-mail addresses for guests to respond whether they're coming or not. So many people in your lives are busy; it may be easier for them to respond by e-mail.

JoEllen and Ben took a photograph of the gorgeous sunset from the deck of the marina country club where they'd be having their wedding and reception, and had it reproduced on their wedding invitation, with a foil seal of the club on the envelope. The invitations were pricey, JoEllen admits, but "they're so beautiful, an aunt has already framed hers and sent it to us as a gift for our home."

JoEllen also included response cards for guests, although she didn't go for the fancier touches like Tammie, preferring to save some money for the music at the reception.

Now for the Flowers!

Weddings and flowers—they just go together. Many of us remember the flowers from weddings we've attended: the fragrant white roses of the bride's bouquet, the garden wedding site that's a symphony of color and scent, the little baskets of lily of the valley at the reception tables.

Flowers can make the wedding. They can also break the budget if you're not careful. How much you choose to spend—and what portion of the budget you allot—is totally up to you. Some sources suggest that flowers and decorations are the second biggest expense after the reception, but you might want that expense to be your wedding gown or some other part of your wedding.

Look at it this way. Are flowers a high priority for you? If not, set a smaller budget for them. Some people are allergic to flowers, so they opt to carry and decorate with silk flowers. Just remember that it can be as expensive to have a florist arrange silks as it is to have fresh flowers.

 ALERT!

Stick to your budget, and be wary of anyone who tries to convince you that you must spend a fortune to get what you want. Careful planning, a willingness to compromise, and sometimes doing things yourself can save you a lot of money.

Choosing a Florist

The best way to be happy with the florist you choose is to get recommendations and referrals from others. Ask the references if the flowers they ended up with were the ones they ordered. Were there any expensive add-ons they hadn't expected? Was the "$99 Special" just a come-on to get them into the florist shop?

Interview the Florist

When you have your preliminary list, try to visit two or three florists before making a choice. Ask lots of questions about what you want, and pay attention to how you're treated. If the florist is not willing to spend a few minutes discussing what you want, you have not found the vendor for you.

Come prepared with pictures of bouquets you like that you've clipped from magazines, and ask if the florist can duplicate the look. If you feel you've been patted on the head and gently encouraged just to choose from a few photos of standard bouquets or a prepackaged floral-arrangement album, you're in the wrong place.

Check Out the Shop

Look around the shop. Do the arrangements in the shop seem like they match your style, or are they too old-fashioned and nothing like the look you had in mind? Can the business realistically accommodate your wedding date? Finally, make certain that all details are put into writing.

Also, make certain that you have a written agreement of the price for the flowers and the style of arrangements. Put in writing when the florist can deliver the flowers for your wedding and reception so that there are no misunderstandings and undelivered flowers.

Ask if the florist will place arrangements and stay

to pin on boutonnieres and corsages. Make certain that the flowers are not just left at the church by the delivery person.

 ESSENTIAL

You can be assured that the money you spend on flowers isn't wasted by getting referrals and recommendations from friends and family. Then check out the florist for yourself before putting down a deposit.

Choosing the Flowers

Many people are all thumbs with flowers and plants and barely know their names. Such people are happy to leave the designing and arranging of them to the florist. Not sure what you want for your bridal bouquet? Don't know what type of flowers would look good or how to describe what you want? Here are some ideas you might like to consider.

A Moderate Way to Save

If you want to save money on flowers and table decorations and feel clueless when it comes to doing things with real and silk flowers, don't despair. Ready-made arrangements are available at many decorating stores; some even have designers who can make up what you want from silk flowers and greenery you purchase at the store.

Check to see if you'll be charged for putting together the arrangement. If there is a charge, it's usually reasonable compared to ordering from a florist. Some florists don't mind mixing silk and real flowers, but the price won't differ much—it's the labor that's usually more expensive than the blooms.

If you live in a bigger city, you can also look into ordering flowers from a wholesaler or visit a flower market or flea market for bargains. Look for locally grown varieties for the best savings.

Handy Flower Guides

One bride went through several issues of bridal magazines for the season she'd be getting married in so that she could get an idea of the kinds of flowers and bouquet shapes that were available. She learned the difference between a cascade bouquet, an arm bouquet (also called presentation bouquet), a nosegay, and so on. This saved her a lot of time when she went to the florist, and kept her from having unrealistic expectations.

"I didn't see certain flowers in the issues, so when I met with the florist, the first question I asked was, why? She explained that they weren't readily available, so I didn't get my heart set on them and then get disappointed."

Since she was having a traditional wedding, the florist showed her an album of bouquets and table arrangements suited to that type of wedding. She knew she had the right florist when the woman urged her to go with a smaller bouquet because she's small in stature. "She explained that I was supposed to be the focal point, not the flowers I carried."

The happy bride also offers another tip: "We also saved having the flowers taken from the church and sent on to the reception site. That was a service that the florist suggested, something I hadn't thought of, and it helped us save the expense of ordering additional flowers for the reception site."

 FACT

Martha Stewart Weddings magazine often features articles showing how to make simple bouquets, demystifying the process and showing you how easy it is to make your own. Check out ✐*www.MarthaStewart.com* and click on "Weddings" for more information on wedding flowers and other features.

"I wanted white roses but didn't want to pay a lot," said Ingrid, a winter bride. "The cost was awful. Then I realized that I could carry one long-stemmed rose wrapped in silk ribbon. The bridesmaids did the same. Guests later told me that we looked so elegant." It's quality—not quantity—that counts!

Special Floral Effects

Weddings that have a medieval, Victorian, or western flavor dictate their own color schemes and flowers. Ivy and wildflowers make good bouquets evocative of Renaissance times, while rose-and-lace nosegays are suitable for a Victorian theme. Western brides take their inspiration from regional flowers and casual bouquet shapes.

A recent medieval wedding featured ivy trailing little porcelain castles at each place setting. For a Victorian-themed wedding, lots of roses and old-fashioned touches such as lace and vintage accessories continue the theme. Western weddings can feature casual bunches of wildflowers tucked into enamelware or splatterware pitchers and bowls—or even cowboy boots!

Small Elements Have Big Appeal

Smaller individual decorations such as votive candles in little glass holders or little glass flowerpots filled with blooms are inexpensive touches that add elegance to any wedding, regardless of budget. For modest budgets, look in dollar stores for cute little glass flowerpots and votives in bundles of one hundred; these items are also on sale at craft stores and discount superstores. For moderate weddings, look in department stores for fancier glass votive holders and candles. For truly lavish weddings, think about bowls with floating candles every few place settings at the table.

Let's see what our three couples chose for their floral arrangements.

Out of the Ordinary

Because of the lavish nature of the wedding and the

elegant setting they were using, JoEllen and Ben wanted something really special.

"We chose orchids for my bouquet, not just because I love them, but because they'll remind me that right after the wedding, we're leaving for our honeymoon in Hawaii," JoEllen explained. "My florist looked at a picture of my gown and suggested orchids. But we didn't need a whole bouquet of them to make a point. An orchid was the centerpiece of a cascade bouquet."

JoEllen's florist carried out the theme of a marina country club wedding with table centerpieces of silver-plated sailboats filled with white roses, and small silver-plated bowls with floating white candles.

 FACT

Weddings that are held during certain seasons such as Christmas give you lots of ideas for inexpensive decorating. An added bonus is that many of the places you'll use for a ceremony or reception site will be decorated for the season, saving you money!

Daisies Do Tell—of Savings

Amanda didn't have to spend a lot of money on her floral budget. "The area we're planning to be married in has so many beautiful flowers and plants. We'll use the daisy-decorated heart to show guests where the wedding is located. And, of course, I need a bouquet, my maid of honor needs one, and we have a flower girl."

Amanda decided on a bouquet of daisies accented with several white and yellow roses. "Something exotic just wouldn't work with what I'm planning to wear," she says. "And the more exotic or out of season, the more expensive."

Since daisies are in season, Amanda will likely get a bargain price on them—at the grocery store! "My aunt will put together white and yellow daisies and roses into simple bouquets for my maid of honor and me. And little baskets of daisies will serve as our reception picnic centerpieces."

Decorating with Flowers

Tammie's florist is planning to use touches of antique-looking lace ribbon on the bridal bouquet and table arrangements. Copies of the pictures that show the bride and groom's families will be featured on the guest-book table.

 ESSENTIAL

Investigate *www.blissezine.com*, a Web site with a floral guide that tells you types of flowers, their colors, and available seasons. It also helps to know what a particular flower is, or what would be a good substitute for something more expensive than your budget will allow.

Don't Forget All the Details

You will need flowers for the setting of your wedding ceremony. Do you want an arrangement for the front of the church? Around a unity candle? What about the pews?

If you're using a large church or synagogue, the flower and ribbon decorations on the pews can really add up. Decide whether you want to have a decoration on each pew, every other pew, and so on. Figure out the costs of simple and elaborate choices, and then you'll know which you want.

Also, don't forget to budget for corsages for the mothers and grandmothers. Many brides order corsages that have flowers similar to those in their bridal bouquets, but if you know either your mother or your fiancé's mother has a special flower she loves, you might want to incorporate it, if it's not too expensive or out of season.

Amanda's love for daisies will be emphasized in not only the bouquets for herself and her attendants, as mentioned earlier, but also in corsages for the mothers and a boutonniere for the best man. Tammie chose pale yellow roses for remembrance in her bouquet, but they wouldn't match the colors worn by the mothers, so she ordered white roses for them.

When Silk Is a Good Idea

Be sure to find out whether any members of your wedding party have an allergy to certain flowers. You don't want to spend all that money and end up with them sneezing and red-eyed on this important day!

"When my mom found out that we were ordering a silk corsage for my mother-in-law, who's allergic to many flowers, she wanted one, too," said a recently married friend. "They look so pretty in little shadow boxes on the wall in their bedrooms."

Boutonnieres can be expensive if you get too fancy with the variety of flowers or with the arrangement. Most men generally prefer just a small, simple flower pinned to their lapel, anyway.

 ALERT!

> If a friend or family member offers to help you with flowers for your wedding, make certain that it's someone who will do what you want, not take off in a direction you don't like.

Make sure that you've arranged for the flowers to be picked up or delivered. A horror story passed around at a wedding shower recently concerned a friend who had a relative who was going to do the flowers, and then her check bounced!

"We didn't find out until the evening before the wedding! We had to scramble to find another alternative at the last minute and was it ever expensive!" related the friend.

And All the Rest

Remember to budget for the touches that make your wedding special. Are you including a flower girl and a ring bearer? Little ones make the wedding so sweet. But items like that fancy ring pillow or the flower girl's basket can really add up.

A Tisket, a Tasket

Tammie wanted a ring bearer but thought that $35 was excessive for the pillow. "My aunt who loves to sew made one from half a yard of satin fabric she found marked down. She used some scraps of vintage lace she already had, and it was darling. It cost $4.98."

"We found a white basket at Wal-Mart, hot-glued silk daisies around the rim, and filled it with silk rose petals for the flower girl," said Amanda. "The cost? Under $10."

JoEllen didn't want a ring bearer or a flower girl. "We plan on having a nice reception dinner and lots of dancing. I don't think most of my friends would want to bring their children. Instead, it will be like a night out for them."

But a unity candle was something she wanted as an extra touch at her wedding. "Everywhere we looked, they were so expensive. Just because I'm spending a lot on the wedding doesn't mean I want to waste money. What were we talking about—a pillar candle and some decoration?"

ESSENTIAL

> Budgeting your time and energy is as important as budgeting your finances. Take care of the minor details as they arise so you don't have lots of loose ends as your wedding approaches.

Instead, JoEllen decided she'd try doing it herself. "I'm what you call 'craft-impaired'—all thumbs. But I figured if I messed up, I'd just lose a few dollars. I found something I could use at a discount store, and then decorated it myself."

Remember that for your invitations and your flowers—as with everything else for your big day—setting your priorities is the first step in determining your budget. Be willing to spend money on what's most important, and be more conservative on the other things.

THE PERSONAL FLORIST PLANNER

FLOWERS FOR THE BRIDE	COST
bridal bouquet	-------------
a smaller bouquet (for the bouquet toss)	-------------
floral headdress	-------------
going-away corsage	-------------

FLOWERS FOR THE BRIDAL ATTENDANTS	COST
matron of honor's bouquet	-------------
maid of honor's bouquet	-------------
bridesmaids' bouquets	-------------
flower girl's bouquet and flower petals	-------------
floral headdresses	-------------

FLOWERS FOR THE GROOM AND HIS ATTENDANTS	COST
groom's boutonniere	-------------
best man's boutonniere	-------------
ushers' boutonnieres	-------------
ringbearer's boutonniere	-------------

continued on page 121

THE PERSONAL FLORIST PLANNER

**FLOWERS FOR THE FAMILY
AND SPECIAL FRIENDS**   COST

bride's mother   _____

groom's mother   _____

other family members   _____

**FLOWERS FOR WEDDING HELPERS
AND PARTICIPANTS**   COST

bridal consultant   _____

officiant   _____

soloist   _____

readers   _____

instrumentalist   _____

guest book attendant   _____

gift attendant   _____

others   _____

**FLOWERS FOR THE
REHEARSAL DINNER**   COST

centerpieces   _____

other   _____

continued on page 123

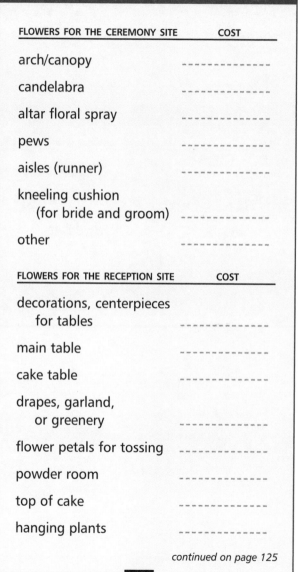

THE PERSONAL FLORIST PLANNER

FLOWERS FOR THE CEREMONY SITE	COST
arch/canopy	------------
candelabra	------------
altar floral spray	------------
pews	------------
aisles (runner)	------------
kneeling cushion (for bride and groom)	------------
other	------------

FLOWERS FOR THE RECEPTION SITE	COST
decorations, centerpieces for tables	------------
main table	------------
cake table	------------
drapes, garland, or greenery	------------
flower petals for tossing	------------
powder room	------------
top of cake	------------
hanging plants	------------

continued on page 125

THE PERSONAL FLORIST PLANNER

FLOWERS FOR THE RECEPTION SITE	COST
small trees	------------
other	------------

FLORIST FEES	COST
deposit fees	------------
delivery charges	------------
other	------------

OTHER FEES	COST
------------------	------------
------------------	------------
------------------	------------
------------------	------------
------------------	------------
------------------	------------

TOTAL: ------------

Music and Transportation

I f flowers scent the air and are a wonder to the eyes, so, too, is music a delight to the senses. Music adds an undeniably special touch to any occasion. It sets the mood and helps make the memories. Transportation to the church and reception can also set a mood, whether you arrive in a limo or on a motorcycle!

Choosing the Type of Music

People might not remember the food they ate at a reception or what the flowers were, but they will remember the music that was playing and what they danced to.

What kind of music do you want at your wedding and reception? Do you love classical music and think harps, violins, and maybe Pachelbel's Canon are the way to go? Maybe your idea of a classic is the old Elvis standby, "Love Me Tender." Perhaps you will choose to have an organist play the traditional wedding march as you proceed down the aisle.

Do You Sing the Same Song?

How alike are your musical interests? Do they coincide or diverge? Sometimes, one person loves classical music and the other enjoys heavy metal. Well, that makes for some interesting conversations—and some interesting choices, especially on your wedding day.

Whichever music you choose, it will be right for you, your fiancé, and your day together. In some locations, only taped music will be available or appropriate, and that's fine. In fact, in some ways, it will make things easier—no worries about the musicians not showing up, or doing a bad job. All you have to do is check to make sure that the sound equipment is functioning, or bring a small tape recorder.

Making sure you find the right musicians for the right price is the next important step in your budget. How important is music in your wedding? How much do you want to budget for it?

Hit the Right Key

Amanda and Dustin lucked out. "I started out thinking that it was going to be hard to have what we wanted with our budget," Amanda says. "I mean, we just don't have that much to work with."

Then, one day when she was walking on campus, it hit her. "There's a music department at our college, and many of the music students hire out for occasions in the community. We have our choice of harpists, violinists, pianists, and organists—you name it! Even a steel band made up of students from the islands!"

What about Something Classical?

They had a long conversation and decided to go with a harpist. "I've always loved the music of a harp," Amanda said. "And the setting seemed perfect for it. We'll seat her under a tree near the reflecting pool, and have her playing when the guests are gathering. Then she'll play during the ceremony, and after, while we have our picnic. I can't imagine anything more elegant."

"Even better was the price," added Dustin. "She gave us a special rate because we're students, and because she's living on campus."

FACT

Most musicians who play events have demo tapes, but those don't give you any idea of how they'll sound live. To hear what they really sound like, you can ask to drop in on an event they're playing before you make your commitment.

If you have a college or university, even a small music school, in your area, this might be a good source for musicians for your wedding and reception (and other types of services, too!). Students are always in need of money for tuition and living expenses, and looking to build experience for their future careers.

Be sure to check the musicians' references and make certain that there is a backup plan in place if they are ill and can't make your event. Also offer to provide a reference for them if you're happy with their work.

Music in the Key of Life

A fan of the traditional, Tammie wanted the wedding standard "Here Comes the Bride" played by the church organist. "I just always dreamed that I'd hear that music when I was walking down the aisle with my father. When I told Matt, he said he wanted me to have that."

It took only a few minutes after church one Sunday to talk with the organist, find out if he could play on the wedding date, and arrange payment details. Tammie is satisfied that the church organist will do a good job—she has heard him play many Sundays and for a fellow church member's wedding.

The Women's Club, where they are thinking about having their reception, has a small stage for a deejay or a band. The more they talked about music, the more Tammie and Matt realized that they had an interesting situation in regard to their theme. They want to honor their parents and grandparents, and what better way than to have music they can dance to.

The deejay said he would play Glenn Miller, Frank Sinatra, the music of the times when their parents and grandparents were getting married. In fact, Tammie and Matt are going to casually ask their parents and grandparents what they danced to on their wedding day—without telling them what they are planning.

What about Deejays?

If you're planning to have a deejay, there are several different ways you can find one. First—always!—ask a friend or coworker if they know one or have seen one at a recent event. That's always a good way to find someone who has shown ability and dependability.

Some deejays advertise in the yellow pages of the phone book, the newspaper, a local weekly shopper, even the bulletin board at the Laundromat.

Finding a Deejay

Rates for deejays can vary widely. Plan on making a number of calls and talking to several deejays to find one who can meet your musical needs and fit your budget.

There are some important questions to ask when interviewing a deejay. First, is he available for your date, and how soon does he need you to commit to it? Second, will you be charged by the job or by the hour? This is really important.

 ESSENTIAL

> Check out a Web site that also will help you find a deejay in your area. Simply click on *www.WeDJ.com* and then click on your state and county. You'll find lists of deejays in your area, with a simple way to contact them and set up arrangements.

If the party really gets going but it's time for the deejay to leave, it might be disappointing for everyone. If, on the other hand, you have a very specific time allotment and then you want things to shut down, a pre-arranged time period might be a good idea.

Will the deejay be able to supply the music that you want? How much time will he need to set up? (You'll need to have someone available to let him into your reception area to do this.) What type of attire does the deejay wear to the function, and is that appropriate for the day you're planning? Does he have a list of his music collection to show you, and how much say do you have in what he plays?

A Deejay as Master of Ceremonies

Some couples choose to have the deejay act as master of ceremonies and announce them and their wedding party as they join the reception. If this is what you want, it needs to be stated ahead of time. Give him a list of the names and how they're pronounced, too.

In Tammie and Matt's case, one deejay seemed particularly well suited to the job. "Even though he was young, he knew all about the musical choices I wanted played for my parents and grandparents to dance to," said Tammie. "He'd played them for other events with older people. Yet he had some suggestions for modern music for us and guests our age. It felt like a match."

They checked out the references the deejay cheerfully supplied and were assured that his previous employers were quite happy with his work. All that remains to be done is sign an agreement of terms that states that if the deejay becomes ill and cannot work the event, he will make certain that another deejay of similar ability will be there on time. That's important to prevent disappointment on your wedding day.

The deejay they chose wasn't the least expensive of the several they interviewed, but they'd heard horror stories from friends who'd hired the deejay with the lowest bid and been very disappointed.

FACT

One couple rented a good stereo system from one of those stores that rents out everything from furniture to washers. A friend burned CDs of their favorite songs, and the music played on without the expense of a deejay!

Then There's Live Music

Are you planning live music for your reception? Although this is not an inexpensive choice, it can be just right for some couples. JoEllen and Ben decided from the moment they started planning that they would be spending a big portion of their wedding budget on the reception.

What Type of Music Do You Need?

"We want a big dinner party for our friends," said JoEllen. "Ben and I love jazz and go to clubs often." The next time they went to a club and listened to their favorite group, Ben approached the musicians on break and asked whether they performed at weddings. He was given the name of their agent and contacted him.

"We were rather shocked at the price, but I talked with JoEllen, and we agreed they were the group we wanted. We'll have them for fewer hours than a deejay, but it's worth the expense. After all, it's for our wedding day!"

How will you use music to make your wedding day

special? What portion of your wedding budget do you want to use for that purpose? Once you answer the first question and agree on where music falls on your list of priorities, the second question will be much easier to address.

Get Me to the Church on Time!

How are you going to get to the wedding and reception? By now you've probably sat down and figured out if you need special transportation to your wedding and reception. Arranging it can be enjoyable, not a challenge, if you remember to use the same planning and budget cautions you've been using with other aspects of your wedding planning.

How Will You Get There?

Do you want to be driven to the church in a limousine? How big a limousine do you need? These vehicles come in sizes from a seating capacity of three up to limousine coaches that seat twenty. There are even SUV limos. If your wedding party is large, you can rent minibuses that seat sixteen, and motor coaches that seat up to forty-eight. You can even charter party buses.

Always get recommendations from friends and family, or, if they haven't used a limousine service lately, ask business associates, and finally your wedding vendors. If you choose to call a limo company advertising in your local phone directory or the newspaper, remember that a big ad doesn't mean quality service.

Check Things Out

Visit the company and talk to a representative about needs and prices, and ask to see their vehicles and a contract. Be sure to ask if any wedding packages are available and what they include.

 ESSENTIAL

Try to have most of your details settled before you draw up a contract. The more specific you can be (times, tolls, number of people—even mileage) up front, the fewer surprises you'll have later.

Most limos are contracted at an hourly rate, which will quickly add up during the ceremony and reception. When does the "time clock" begin—when the car leaves the garage, or when it arrives at your house? Could overtime be involved? If you live in a large city, there may be tolls and parking charges, too. Who pays for those? Be sure all these points are included in your contract. Additional charges to budget for include a gratuity, which can sometimes be as high as 20 percent.

Tying Down the Details

With more companies leasing their vehicles, it will

be important to know who actually owns the limo. Who will be responsible if the transportation doesn't work as planned on your important day?

Make sure the contract specifies all information important to you, not just the name of the limo company. Include details such as what time you must be picked up, how many people will be riding in the vehicle, and so on. Also specify in the contract the exact type of car you need, so that you don't get something smaller than or not as nice as what you wanted.

Other Choices

Limousines aren't the only type of transportation available. City transportation companies sometime lease local tourist trolleys. A driver wearing a period trolley-driver's uniform picks up the guests and takes them on a scenic drive to their destination.

The trip often turns into an occasion of its own as riders enjoy the ambiance of this unique ride. Charges compare to a motor coach rented by limo companies. For a different look, consider renting antique cars or unusual vehicles such as Humvees.

Tammie and Matt decided to take a romantic horse-drawn carriage ride to their reception site just a few blocks away from the church where they were married. They felt it would make for a nice transition from one place to the other, and would allow them some private time together as newlyweds. Their contract includes a bottle of champagne and a tuxedoed driver.

A Limo-less Solution

"We don't need a limo," says Amanda, "but I don't want to crush my dress driving there in my little compact car. So I asked a college friend if he'd be willing to drive me in his big Lincoln, and he was delighted to help. He wouldn't take any money; he said he enjoyed being asked to a picnic lunch outside on such a pretty day.

 ALERT!

> Be mindful of the parking situation at your reception site. If your guests will have a difficult time finding the site or parking near it, consider chartering a bus to shuttle all guests from the wedding site.

When a Limo's What You Want

Tammie hired a limousine to transport her and her wedding party to the church. "My parents and I want to go together—it will be very special, being with them just before I am married."

JoEllen will drive to the marina country club in a limousine, and then she and Ben will take it to the airport for their flight to Hawaii.

ESSENTIAL

> If you're serving alcohol at your reception, have a member of your wedding party stay alert for anyone who looks as if he or she needs a safe ride home. This is a duty the groom might ask his best man to unobtrusively perform.

What about Specialty Transportation?

Wedding transportation can be as different—and fun—as you want it to be. If it's a medieval wedding you have in mind, could you hire horses or a horse-drawn carriage? For a western wedding, horses seem a must, or perhaps there is a horse-drawn wagon available for hire in your area. Some people choose a motorcycle as their mode of wedding transportation. Couples have even taken hot-air balloons to their receptions.

When making your plans, consider that the most important thing is that you get to where you're going on time. Beyond that, your transportation choices are limited by only your wedding budget and your imagination!

Chapter 9
Picture This!

You want to capture the memories from your wedding—but you don't want to throw away dollars on that picture of you throwing your bouquet! Here's how to choose the right photographer and get the photo album you want without sacrificing your budget.

Determining Your Needs

What kind of photography package do you need? Are you looking for shots of the wedding and reception to fill a large keepsake album and have copies made for your family, or will a small album and a few 5-by-7-inch photographs for your parents and wedding party serve your needs?

The package deal that you make with your photographer can be as big—or as small—as you want it to be. A friend or family member could take your photographs for free, or you could hire a team of photographers that will charge you thousands of dollars for its services.

 ALERT!

Don't fall into the trap of feeling that you're obligated to give out lots of your wedding pictures to your family and your wedding party. You're sure to make the photography portion of your budget rise to the levels of the national debt!

Do you like candid shots or more formal portraits? These days, couples seem to like a combination. Few people want a collection of nothing but silly shots that might have seemed humorous at the time but don't reflect the serious commitment made that day.

What about black and white or color? Black and white might seem very traditional to some people, trendy to others, depending on how the photographs are taken. You might prefer color to really show the glow of ivory candlelight, the colors of the flowers in your bouquet, or the brilliant sunset as you leave the reception. Perhaps a combination of the two will fit into your photography budget.

Save with a Smaller Album

Is an album of wedding photographs one of the high-priority items in your wedding budget? If it isn't, then scale down the number of shots taken and photographs developed and how many hours you contract for.

For a modest budget, choose a less ornate album and fewer posed shots that take a lot of time to compose. Decide how much time you want the photographer to spend at the ceremony and reception, and plan accordingly. Package size and complexity of shots can increase with the portion of the budget you're using.

Shop Around

The first place to start your search is where you've started with so many other decisions—recommendations from friends and family who have used a photographer recently. Look at their photographs and albums and ask about how the photographer did the work that day. Here are a few sample questions:

1. Did the photographer show up on time?
2. Did the photographer dress appropriately?

3. Did the photographer bring enough film for all the shots without having to scramble to get some more?
4. Did the photographer capture all the important parts of the ceremony and the reception?

Make sure that the quality of photographs and the type of shots match what you are looking for.

Ask your friends and family members if they mind telling you what prices they paid for their wedding photography and if proofs were delivered when expected—and listen carefully when you ask if there was pressure to buy more than they wanted or if they couldn't get a big group shot because the photographer insisted smaller groups would be better (thus more pictures to buy!).

 ESSENTIAL

> Choosing to take fewer pictures does not mean that you need to settle for a mediocre photographer. After all, these are important photographs that can't be taken again. Think about it this way: If there are minor mishaps that day, they probably won't be remembered. But a photograph is forever.

Check with your other vendors, too, because they may have worked with both good and not-so-good photographers. Your officiant also may be a good source of information on photographers if he or she performs a lot of weddings.

One bride reported that her minister was very unhappy to hear that a particular photographer had been chosen. At a previous wedding, the photographer had been late and held everyone up, and he'd taken shots at inappropriate times. The minister reported that the bridal couple had later told him they'd been very unhappy with his work and his hard-sell approach to persuade them to buy more photos than their agreed-upon package. Fortunately, a deposit hadn't been put down yet, so the bride-to-be could make an agreement with a different photographer.

Speak with the Photographer

Make an appointment with at least two photographers, so you can view their samples and get a sense of how your requests are viewed. If you sense at all that your discussion is not what you expected, it's best to look elsewhere. You're not likely to get any happier with a person who can't make a good impression the first time around. Be sure that you're comfortable with the person you're hiring—they'll be with you, often in close quarters, for hours on your special day.

Be sure to ask the photographer about how he or she will dress for your wedding. "I spent so much time and money trying to make sure that I had an elegant wedding," said one bride. "Then this photographer shows up in a polo shirt and khakis to take the wedding pictures. We were mortified!"

Ask if the photographer does this work full time or if it's a weekend or a part-time occupation. There's absolutely nothing wrong with part-time photographers, but be even more careful to check their references and portfolios.

 ALERT!

> Sometimes ritzy studios rely on the name of one photographer but use a staff of others. Ask to see *your* photographer's portfolio—you may be paying for a better photographer than you'll get!

It's essential that you determine that the person you're talking to is the one who'll be your photographer later. Interviewing and developing a relationship with someone besides *your* photographer could create a lot of miscommunication and disappointment—not to mention a difference in the quality from what you expected.

Cast a Wide Net

You need not always restrict yourself to professional photographers. If someone in your family wants to take the photos, accept their offer—that is, if you truly believe they can do a great job. This occasion is too important to risk getting an amateur.

And here is another idea: Think locally! Many colleges and universities have photography departments or actual schools of photography. You may be able to locate a skilled instructor or student who does weddings.

Additional Questions

Whether you use a full-time professional or someone else, additional questions to ask your photographer are:

1. Can we see samples of photography done at weddings like ours? What type of camera will you use? What type of shot do you consider your specialty?
2. Do you (the photographer or the studio) offer packages? How much time will you spend working at our wedding? (You don't want to be billed for overtime.)
3. Do you offer digital photography? (This saves money over traditional photography.)
4. Can we keep the negatives? (If not, ask how long you or others have to order other pictures.) When will our proofs be available? Will you be supplying the album?
5. How far ahead do we need to confirm your time? (Bear in mind that during especially busy periods such as the holidays and the peak bridal months, you may need to reserve your date far ahead.)
6. How much of a deposit is required? May we see a copy of the contract?

A Checklist of Posing Shots

Once you have picked your photographer, you should also be sure to discuss posing shots. Decide ahead of time which shots you'll want and when you want them. Point out those types of shots you particularly like, and be sure that the photographer knows what kind you dislike.

 ESSENTIAL

> Even if you are on a luxurious budget, don't go overboard with photography. Remember, it's your wedding, not a photo op! Don't spend too much time standing around having your picture taken.

Has the photographer taken shots similar to the type you want—and in a similar location to the one in which you're being married? You've carefully chosen your wedding and reception sites for a reason—if they're particularly beautiful or spiritual, you want that reflected in your photographs.

A New Trend

Pre-wedding shots are a new trend. Some couples, eager to keep guests from having to sit around while wedding party shots are being taken, prefer to have the photography done before the ceremony begins.

One bride thought she wouldn't like having her picture taken with her fiancé before the ceremony but changed her mind after she did it. "We had the chance to be with a very small number of people we loved and see each other for the first time that day," she said. "It was so emotional for both of us. I'm glad we did it."

A Place to Start

Consider the following sampling of some traditional photographs chosen by the bridal couple:

Portraits: Portrait photographs might contain the following:

- ❑ The bride
- ❑ The bride and groom
- ❑ The bride with her maid of honor and bridesmaids
- ❑ The groom with his best man and/or groomsmen
- ❑ The ring bearer and the flower girl
- ❑ The bride with her parents
- ❑ The groom with his parents
- ❑ The bride and groom with each set of parents
- ❑ The bride and groom with both sets of parents
- ❑ The entire wedding party

The Ceremony: Ceremony shots might include the following:

- ❑ The location outside of the ceremony site
- ❑ Special guests and the bride and groom's parents being seated by the ushers

- ❏ The groom walking down the aisle
- ❏ The groom, ushers, and the maid or matron of honor and the bridesmaids waiting at the altar
- ❏ The flower girl and/or ring bearer walking down the aisle
- ❏ The bride walking down the aisle
- ❏ The wedding kiss
- ❏ The bride and groom leading the recessional
- ❏ Guests tossing birdseed or flower petals as the bride and groom leave the ceremony location

Ⓔ ALERT!

Avoid potential embarrassment by alerting your photographer to any awkward situations. For instance, if your parents are divorced and not speaking to each other, the photographer shouldn't try to group them together in a shot with the bride and groom.

The Reception: Reception shots might include the following:

- ❏ People signing the guest book
- ❏ The best man, maid of honor, parents, or others offering a toast
- ❏ The bride and groom as they listen to the toasts
- ❏ Pictures of those seated at the tables
- ❏ The bride and groom's first dance
- ❏ The bride and her father dancing

❏ The groom and his mother dancing
❏ The cake
❏ The bride and groom as they cut the cake
❏ The bride and groom as they leave for their honeymoon

Behind-the-Scenes: Other important shots include the following:

❏ The bride and groom as they get dressed, with or without their attendants or parents
❏ The bride pinning on her father's boutonniere
❏ The mother helping the bride with her dress or veil
❏ The bride and groom as they each leave for the ceremony

If photographs of the wedding party are being taken before the ceremony, ask the photographer to take special care to catch that first moment when the bride and groom see each other. The two close-up shots (one of the bride and one of the groom) are considered by most people to be the most memorable ones, and you will probably want them no matter what size the wedding photograph package is.

Candid Shots

In looking through either the photographer's portfolio or albums or proofs of recently married friends, you may notice that the candid shots capture more than posed portraits. Although it's always good to plan what you want, if you have the right photographer, you should be able to trust his judgment.

 ESSENTIAL

> Let your photographer know that if he or she sees a really great casual shot that it's okay to snap it—some of those end up being the most memorable ones. That candid of the four-year-old flower girl or your grandparents dancing might just say it all.

Some Alternatives

There are some good reasons for not having a photographer at your wedding. Some people have a small, intimate wedding with just a few family members and/or friends and don't want the intrusion of an outsider on their special day. Some people just can't find a photographer within their limited budget. Other couples are simply uncomfortable with photographers popping up here and there and snapping shots.

A nice alternative is having a portrait done in a studio. These shots are done in a controlled setting, with particularly good lighting and without the weather and time constraints of ceremony and reception locations. There are just the three of you–the bride, the groom, and the photographer; no one else sees or hears how the shots are set up.

Special moments between the bride and groom as they gaze at each other, for instance, can be very intimate; neither needs to feel pressured by onlookers. If either of you has ever been unhappy with the way posed or candid shots have turned out—"Oh, no, I don't look like that, do I?"—then a studio portrait can be a great alternative.

Your Guests Can Take Great Shots, Too!

Another great alternative is to hand out disposable cameras to a number of people at the wedding and reception. They may see special shots that the professional photographer doesn't or, just by the act of taking that picture, show you what moments at the wedding were particularly meaningful to them. (Do put a cautionary note on the cameras if your church or synagogue does not want photos taken during the ceremony.)

 FACT

Instead of having a guest book, one couple had a favorite picture of themselves blown up and mounted on posterboard. It sat on a table at the wedding, where guests signed around the picture. The couple had it mounted and framed for their first home together.

Having your guests do informal photography can also help you save money. Some couples have a professional photographer for the ceremony and use the informal shots guests take at the reception for their album. The choice is yours!

From a Kid's Point of View

Older children enjoy using inexpensive disposable cameras to record a child's-eye view of the wedding and reception. These pictures, while not always of the quality of those taken by adults, can be charming and will give children the opportunity to be part of things. Later, you can put the photos into frames and present them as gifts.

Getting It on Video

Are you interested in having your wedding and reception videotaped? Some couples do. It's a fad that became a trend, and now more couples are adding this service to their wedding. As video cameras become more popular and are priced more affordably, more people have started recording their special events.

And the Oscar Goes to . . .

Of course, wedding tapes run the gamut from choppy homemade videos to master works of art worthy of an Oscar nomination. Prices vary widely as well, from the hundreds to the thousands. With this kind of expenditure and the importance of the video being done just as well as your photographs, it's important to look carefully for a good videographer.

Recommendations can come from the same people you asked about photographers. In addition, you can ask your photographer to recommend a videographer because in the course of photographing weddings, he or she has undoubtedly met several.

 QUESTION?

What are the benefits of having your wedding videotaped?
Simply put, a videographer will produce a video so you can watch your wedding and reception again and again to relive that special day. If friends or family were unable to come, it's a great way to show them what happened.

Choosing a Videographer

Ask to see a sample of the prospective videographer's work; find out what kind of equipment he or she will bring to the wedding, whether sound will be recorded, and if the video will be edited. Will you be able to copy the video, or is it made so that you can't do this?

Beware of well-intentioned but inexperienced family members who have just bought a new videotape recorder and can't wait to use it. Sure, they can bring it to the wedding and make a video for themselves, but do you really want to rely on Uncle Joe for your wedding video? Is it really a good idea? Only you know the answer to that question.

And what about that friend who graduated from film school and can't wait to be the next Hitchcock or Scorcese? In such a case, you should ask yourself, what are the chances that my wedding video will look like a scene from *Psycho* or *The Godfather*?

Just as when you are deciding whether to take up a relative or a friend on an offer to photograph your wedding, you should ask yourself if the quality of the video will be as good as that done by a professional. If that quality will be there, then you have your videographer, probably for the price of the videotape.

Three Possible Scenarios

Amanda and Dustin found a student photographer who does weddings on the weekends, but they decided that a video wasn't for them. "It just felt like too much for such a small outdoor wedding."

Tammie and Matt do want a video of their wedding. They found a photographer and a videographer based on the recommendation of friends who'd been married recently. "We think it'll be wonderful to have a video to look at later."

JoEllen and Ben shopped carefully for their photographer but decided against a videographer, preferring to spend the money on the jazz band that is to be featured at their reception.

PHOTOGRAPHER BUDGET WORKSHEET

SERVICE	COST
photographer fee (based on hourly rate or prearranged payment)	....
overtime fees	....
travel fees	....
custom-paging fee	....
album-inscription fee	....
additional wedding albums (for parents)	....
engagement session fees	....
rehearsal dinner fees	....
additional photo session fees	....
cost of film, proofing, and processing	....
amount of deposit	....
other	....
	....
	....

continued on page 159

PHOTOGRAPHER BUDGET WORKSHEET

ADDITIONAL PHOTOGRAPHS	COST
11-by-14 portraits	- - - - - - - - - - - - -
8-by-10 portraits	- - - - - - - - - - - - -
5-by-7 prints	- - - - - - - - - - - - -
4-by-5 prints	- - - - - - - - - - - - -
3-by-5 prints	- - - - - - - - - - - - -
wallet-sized prints	- - - - - - - - - - - - -
other prints	- - - - - - - - - - - - -
	- - - - - - - - - - - - -
	- - - - - - - - - - - - -
	- - - - - - - - - - - - -
	- - - - - - - - - - - - -
TOTAL:	- - - - - - - - - - - - -

CHAPTER 10

Remember the Extras

It's the little touches that people remember—the things you do that make them know you're so glad that they came to help you celebrate your marriage and to see you begin a new life with the one you love. But little things add up and can break your budget, so take the advice of that old saying: Watch the pennies and the dollars will take care of themselves.

Wedding Favors and Frills

Wedding favors are such a nice touch to a wedding reception. They may be used at the wedding or reception—like a tulle-wrapped packet of rice or birdseed to throw at the bridal couple (take off the tulle, of course!).

Other times, they are a decorative touch to a reception table; still others, a small but heartfelt gift for your guests to take home. If you have a wedding with a fairy-tale, country, or medieval flavor to it, favors can be fun and fairly inexpensive to think up.

 QUESTION?

Do you know where the idea of wedding favors began?
In medieval times, knots made of ribbon would be attached to a bride's dress and torn off by guests in a spirited contest for a trophy. Sometimes charms were baked into the wedding cake.

Favors for Your Budget

Favors can be as small in size as a little bag of candy or as big as—well, as big as your budget will allow. They can be as inexpensive as a votive candle or as pricey as a sterling Tiffany bud vase engraved with the names of the bride and groom and the date of the wedding. It's up to you—and your budget—to decide what you want to do.

Once you decide, stay firm with your choice. It's too easy to add this and add that because you don't feel you're spending much money, until, suddenly, you've spent three times what you budgeted.

Plenty of Room for Creativity

Here is a popular favor idea: Small frames with the names of guests, which you use as place cards at the wedding, serve double duty as favors. These may be purchased at craft supply stores, craft departments in discount stores, party stores, on the Internet, and so on. They can be as simple and inexpensive as the ones you find at the dollar store or as fancy as brocade-covered or silver frames. Check to see if you can get a discount for buying these in bulk in stores or from sources on the Internet.

Small candles make a lovely gift that can again be as inexpensive or expensive as you wish. Wrap one in a circle of tulle and tie it with ribbons the color of your flowers or wedding party dresses, and it makes a lovely gift. Again, those candles may be purchased in bulk.

 ESSENTIAL

Depending on what type you choose, you can either place your favors in a basket at the reception so that guests may take them as they leave, or, if you are having a sit-down dinner, you can place them at the reception tables.

So Many Ideas Are out There

Just mention the words "wedding favors" and everyone you meet has a suggestion. Many ideas await you on the Internet, too. Type "wedding favors" into a search engine, and dozens and dozens of sites will appear—you'll find some sites that offer merchandise at competitive prices and other sites that offer ideas and advice on how to make your own wedding favors. Message boards are another great place to find really unique ideas.

A bride searching for favors for what she termed her Cinderella wedding found a suggestion for chocolate mice made of Hershey's kisses that looked darling on her reception tables. Another bride loved the idea of having little silver bells as favors for the guests. One found a company that sold ribbon streamers to throw at the bridal couple, and they turned out to be a hit at her wedding.

The selection of candy favors is endless. There are companies that make wrappers printed with whatever message you wish; you can use these wrappers to enclose a piece of chocolate. Another way of personalizing candies is to order lollipops decorated with a bride and groom, or have the bride and groom's names printed on the lollipop wrappers.

Love nature? Couples can give tiny tree seedlings with a card telling their guests how to plant them, and know that something from their day will grow in the years to come. Flower seeds are also popular favors. Some companies print the names of the bride and groom and their wedding date on packets of seeds such as forget-me-nots or wildflowers. When the seeds sprout, the guests enjoy pretty blooms and remember the day you were married. Another unusual offering is butterflies, which you can purchase from companies advertised in bridal magazines and on the Internet.

 ALERT!

> Don't feel you have to out-do the last wedding you went to with your favors. If you're creative, and have the time, great! Go for it and make something that only you can do. No time and all thumbs at crafts? That's okay, too! You'll find plenty of ideas for favors that come ready-made.

Make Your Own Favors

Do you like to make crafts? Personalize gifts for special friends? Do people tell you that you always know just the perfect present for them? Then maybe you (and your fiancé?) want to make the favors for your reception yourself, or invite a few friends to help you and make it a party. Or perhaps you have a friend or relative who would like to make your favors.

Potpourri wrapped in tulle or placed in little boxes can be a sweet-smelling favor for guests to take home and enjoy for months to come. It comes in many scents and costs just a few dollars a bag—or you can make your own from flower petals found in your own garden and some scented oils.

 ESSENTIAL

> Check out a local organization that assists mentally or physically challenged people with a chance to work. They may offer assembly services to make your favors for a good price.

Decorative soaps are a great gift, too, and cost little in time and effort to make. Molds and materials are available in most craft stores. Find a pretty pastel-colored soap or two, wrap it in tulle, and tie with a ribbon and maybe a silk flower, and you have a great wedding favor.

A gold or silver craft pen can be used to inscribe the names of the bride and groom and date of the wedding on inexpensive votive candle holders or wine glasses found at a houseware supply store or a dollar store. There are also kits to do faux engravings on the glass. A design of dots, scrolls, or a line from a poem would be a creative touch on the holders or the glasses.

Candle Favors

A scented votive candle is a simple but elegant favor when placed in a little glass holder and wrapped with tissue or tulle and tied with ribbon. Later, when guests burn the candle, they'll remember your wedding!

Inexpensive champagne glasses and some of the new scented gel candle wax can make a beautiful wedding favor. Tint the gel until you get the color of champagne, then fill the glass, and stir to create air bubbles that will look like champagne bubbles. Then just insert a wick, and you have a candle that looks like a glass of the bubbly! It's perfect as a decoration on the reception table, and guests will love to take it home.

Candies and Chocolates

The easiest wedding favor to make, and the one you should really consider making (or asking someone to make for you), is a candy favor. These can be a handful of colorful mints, foil-wrapped chocolates, anything you think your guests would like.

Jordan almonds are a favorite at weddings around the world and come in white, pastel colors, black, even silver and gold (the latter two are foils wrapped around the white almonds). The almonds supposedly are a symbol of life, the sugared coating said to be a wish that the bride and groom will have more sweetness than bitterness in their lives together.

 FACT

Wrap five almonds in a tulle circle, twist, and tie a ribbon around the bundle. The number is symbolic: It represents health, wealth, happiness, fertility, and longevity.

Hershey's kisses are always popular—who can resist chocolate in any form? Simply wrap a few chocolates in tulle just like the almonds, or place them in a little favor box. Favor boxes come in more shapes and sizes and prices than you can imagine, including a little white paper box that looks like a take-out container from a Chinese restaurant.

Wedding Party Gifts

They've been there for you through good times and bad. If you're the bride, they've gone with you to find just the perfect dress and shoes and graciously agreed to do so many things to help you make this wedding possible. If you're the groom, they've been your buddies when you needed someone to listen, and maybe helped you know it was time to take the plunge. Maybe they helped you find a tux that didn't make you look like a refugee from a high school prom.

They're your wedding party. And you want to find something special to thank them for all they've done— and will be doing that day. Just as with everything else in this book, you need to decide on how much you can spend, and if that's not a lot, remember that the thought and care that you use to choose the gift mean more than the bucks spent.

Two Categories of Gifts

Wedding gifts fall into two categories—those that will be used on the day of the wedding and at other dress-up occasions, and those that are everyday useful items. Deciding on the category is as important as how much you'll spend. Do you want your attendants to have something to complete their outfits that day (and keep jewelry coordinated), or do you want them to have something to keep, something that perhaps is not related to the wedding? It's up to you.

For Female Attendants

Gifts in the first category for the maid or matron of honor and the bridesmaids can be jewelry, evening handbags (depending on the time of day of your wedding), dressy headbands, and wraps such as cashmere or chiffon stoles.

For jewelry, you could choose pearl or gold or silver stud earrings, or hoop earrings, or earring and necklace sets made of gems (faux or real) that match their gowns. Bracelets are a little trickier to buy because wrist sizes vary.

 ALERT!

If you choose to buy items that you'll want to have engraved, remember to allow enough time so you don't have to run around picking them up just before the wedding.

If you want something with more everyday use in mind, look for jewelry that can be worn for work or casual dress. Prices for simple earrings can range from under ten to hundreds of dollars. Buying similar items for all the members of the wedding party is probably best—you'll avoid gift envy!

Other thoughtful everyday gifts include baskets filled with items to pamper, such as aromatherapy candles, foaming bath salts, fancy bath sponges, manicure sets, a novel to read in the tub, and after-bath body lotion. These can be bought ready-made, or you can put them together yourself, using items that fit your budget.

A glass vase (or crystal, if you want to spend more) is a great gift that can be used for a blossom at home or at the office every day. Personalize it with a gold or silver craft pen, or use a kit to do faux engraving on the glass. A little frame with a picture of the two of you is a nice present from one friend to another, or you could give a small, elegant photo album, especially the kind made of velvet with a silver frame for a picture on the cover.

For Male Attendants

A traditional gift that grooms have given their groomsmen is a set of cuff links; decide if this is something that the recipient will wear later before you buy them. A men's manicure set or small travel bag might be a good gift.

Additional Unisex Ideas

Gift certificates to the local gym (if, in fact, the attendants are local and enjoy athletic activities), CDs of the wedding and reception music that you can make at home if you have a CD burner, fancy pen-and-pencil sets, business-card holders that have digital clocks and timers built in, Day-Timers or address books, fancy travel mugs, even a silver-plated computer mouse that can be monogrammed.

Then There's Mom and Dad and . . .

Sometimes the bride and groom buy gifts for the parents and grandparents. A number of companies offer monogrammed handkerchiefs for men and women; grandmothers especially would treasure an old-fashioned lace-trimmed handkerchief with the names of the bride and groom and their wedding date embroidered on them.

Silver frames can be ordered with "Daddy's Little Girl" and the like engraved on them, to hold a picture of the bride as a little girl and then as a young woman on her wedding day. Pictures of the bride or groom with parents or grandparents that are put into nice frames will always be a thoughtful, priceless gift.

Tips and Fees

If the officiant of your wedding ceremony is a church official, find out the fee you'll be expected to pay. Don't assume that officiating at your wedding is part of their salary because they're employees of the church or synagogue. Weddings are not considered to be part of regular duties, and the officiant should be compensated.

Don't Skimp Here

If the officiant doesn't want to name a figure, don't assume it's something like twenty dollars for performing this important service that will end up taking several hours of his or her time. Ask some friends or family members who have been recently married what they paid. Think about what an important role this person is performing for you. If a fee is not accepted, then make an appropriate donation to the church or synagogue.

Civil officials who perform a wedding may not be allowed to charge for their services. Check before the wedding to see if there is a fee and how much it is.

 ALERT!

Budget for the marriage license fees, and be sure to plan for the expenses of a blood test or any other requirements that exist in your city and state. Don't be taken by surprise when you find out the price of your wedding license or the waiting period in your area. Check out the information early.

A Tip to the Wise

You also need to thank all the people who helped make your wedding special: caterers or others in charge of your reception, wait staff, bartenders, delivery people, those in charge of flowers, the photographer, the video-grapher, deejays, band members, limo drivers—well, you get the idea. All the appreciation can add up to a lot of tips. Which means an amount you need to budget that maybe you hadn't been thinking about, right?

Wait a minute, you say. I can see tipping some people like the wait staff. But the bridal consultant and the photographer and people like that? Do I need to tip them as well? Well, if they give extra-good service—yes! The general rule is 10 to 15 percent of the total charge and up to 20 percent if the service has been exceptional.

If there are coatroom and powder room attendants, don't forget to include them as well. Check with the manager of the facility to determine proper tipping for this service in your local area.

 ESSENTIAL

If you feel that particular vendors provided excellent service, don't just thank them and tip them. Think about writing them a note or letting them know that you'll be happy to give them a recommendation or reference. It's nice to be appreciated, and doubly nice to know that hard work pays off in future business!

Wedding Insurance 101

You don't want to think about it. But it has to be said. Things happen. That's why many couples consider wedding insurance these days. After all, people have acknowledged that travel insurance is a good idea because everyone's heard a horror story about some poor soul paying all that money for a trip—only to get sick the night before the flight and miss the entire thing. And nobody ever disputes the benefits of car insurance.

A wedding is actually one of the biggest investments you will ever make; many couples spend more on their wedding than they would for an automobile or a trip abroad. Logically, then, wedding insurance might be a good idea.

Will You Be Protected?

True, you've been charging everything on a credit card so that you have resource in case anything happens, and you've signed contracts putting every agreement about goods and services in writing—and that's great. However, those steps won't get your money back if something unforeseen happens.

Imagine the worst-case scenario: Your wedding and reception have to be cancelled because one of you falls ill; your wedding gown or his custom-made tuxedo is lost or damaged; a hurricane or other bad weather requires you to postpone the wedding; one of you is called up for active duty; a vendor doesn't supply your wedding cake; the wedding rings are lost or damaged—any number of things could go wrong.

If you're having the wedding and reception at a private home, you may want to get insurance in case someone is injured or there is damage to property (the homeowner's insurance policy may cover it if you choose not to buy wedding insurance). Did you know that some reception sites require you to carry wedding insurance? Now do you see why this coverage may be a good idea?

Contact your insurance agent for quotes, or look up wedding insurance companies on the Internet. Costs vary. You'll have to decide if it's worth the extra money (possibly a few hundred dollars for a wedding in the five figures), and you'll need to include the cost in your budget to protect your investment. The more you spend on your wedding, the better idea wedding insurance may be.

CHAPTER 11
Budgeting for the Unexpected

Budgeting for the unexpected is making sure you are prepared to handle *anything*. Something you hadn't planned on suddenly needs to be factored into a budget you thought was set. Now what? Here are some ideas that will help you save money and time.

Miscellaneous Expenses

Just what are miscellaneous expenses? The word "miscellaneous" may refer to a number of things. We tend to think of it as every little thing that you didn't think you needed to budget for—all the unexpected stuff that happens when you're engaging in financial planning. Just like in your monthly budget.

Miscellaneous expenses shouldn't take up more than a small amount of your budget. Opinions on their proportion in the budget range from 2 to as much as 12 percent, in part depending on what you consider a miscellaneous expense.

Yet, miscellaneous expenses are not really taken seriously by couples until they add things up. Five percent of a total wedding budget of $16,000 is a hefty $800. You and your fiancé might not have even thought about setting that much aside for something that sounds so small in terms of item importance or in terms of the 5 percent.

Tell Me What They Are

What are some miscellaneous expenses you should be prepared for? Here's a partial list of miscellaneous expenses:

1. Marriage license fees
2. Blood tests that may be required in your state
3. Emergency supplies like a first-aid kit and extra pantyhose for the wedding day
4. Favors

5. Tips and gratuities
6. Transportation expenses related to wedding errands

One way to lighten the load of miscellaneous expenses is to sit down with your fiancé and agree on purchases that you'll make, and when you'll let the other person know that you made them. A budget can stand a few $10 expenditures without a lot of stress, but if each of you is spending $100 and then reporting it, all of a sudden the budget is getting out of control.

One couple that was using a wedding checking account ran into trouble because they didn't sit down and balance the checkbook together. "We nearly bounced a check because he paid for something and didn't write it down," said Dawn. "Then I wrote a big check, and just happened to think to talk to him about it. We looked at each other, and then grabbed the checkbook to figure things out and see if we had enough money to cover everything until we made another deposit!"

 QUESTION?

What do you consider a miscellaneous expense?
Discuss this question with your fiancé. It's an important way to understand spending styles. If one of you thinks numerous small expenses are "no big deal" and the other does—it's a big deal that needs to be discussed!

A Result of Change in Plans

Sometimes the miscellaneous budget can get overdrawn if there is a last-minute change of plans. If you're doing something with your planning that can be "iffy," like having an outdoor wedding in a season where showers are unpredictable, you'll have to provide for an alternate solution, and this could involve miscellaneous expenses.

Some couples rent or buy a large number of umbrellas to keep on hand, or decide to rent a tent, then realize that they didn't include this under the original reception venue expense and stick it in miscellaneous. So there's suddenly a big blip in the miscellaneous category!

Is It Time for Help?

A bridal consultant can be a great help in stemming the tide of miscellaneous expenses. Since they've "seen it all" in their years of wedding planning experience, they can warn you about budget pitfalls such as oozing miscellaneous expenses. Even if you decide not to use a bridal consultant, if you're overwhelmed with planning because of unforeseen work obligations or other responsibilities, you might decide as a last minute thing to hire a consultant to help you on your wedding day.

Planning for Special Needs

Will any of your wedding guests need special arrangements? These days, with people living longer, you may be lucky to have both your grandparents and your great-grandparents in attendance at your wedding. Think about how special that is—to have them there, watching you on your wedding day?

 FACT

> Most buildings conform to the federal and state laws that require modifications for handicapped people, but pay attention to the unique needs of friends and family who will be attending your wedding and reception. You want to give them a good time, not cause them problems.

Consider Special Touches

If you, your fiancé, a member of your wedding party, or someone among your guests is hearing-impaired, think about hiring an interpreter to help with access to the spoken word. It's an incredibly thoughtful thing to do in terms of letting the hearing-impaired individual "hear" your vows and other important things said that day. But even more, there is beauty and eloquence in words being interpreted with the graceful motion of hands, which many people—nonhearing impaired as well as hearing impaired—like to watch.

You can contact your local interpreting agency or deaf and hard-of-hearing community association for names of interpreters you can hire for your occasion, but it may well be that someone in your circle of friends and family is able to serve as an interpreter, especially if the hearing-impaired person is a family member.

A printed program of your ceremony is a wonderful way for your guests to follow along, especially if there are hearing-impaired guests there. Even those who don't have a hearing problem enjoy seeing an order of service so they can be better informed. And you can have the same person who is doing your wedding invitations prepare these programs.

Do you have a family member or friend who is disabled and will have a difficult time getting around at the wedding and reception sites? Consider asking a member of the wedding party or another person you know well to be available to help. If special transportation is needed and you know that without it, this person will not be able to attend the wedding, then think about arranging that—especially if you know that the cost would be prohibitive for his or her budget.

 QUESTION?

Are any of your guests vegetarian?
Even if there aren't any strict vegetarians at your gathering, people might not eat a particular type of meat and will appreciate your thinking of them. Children who attend will also appreciate having something they like to eat and drink.

Will there be guests with special dietary needs, restrictions, or allergies? Be very careful to honor their requests for substitutions or special arrangements when planning your food and drink. You're a poor host if you discount the importance of their requests!

Be sure to tell your caterer of these needs well in advance, as they may entail more work than you realize. Ask if there is any additional charge, and put all of this information into your agreement for the entire food-and-drink package.

If Something Goes Wrong

There are hundreds of things that can go wrong. Step back, take a deep breath, assess, and then decide what you need to do. Above all, don't panic. There are worse things that can happen than to have some arrangement for your wedding go awry.

Maybe you got downsized, laid off—or fired. Or it happened to your fiancé. Maybe one of you is called up for military service. Or maybe there's been a death in the family, and you feel that you can't go through with the celebration.

Don't despair. First off, you've got that wedding insurance, right? If it's something big that threatens your wedding day—as a hurricane in South Carolina did a few years ago—then you just have to be realistic and remember what's important.

If it's a financial crunch you're facing, downsize your planning and expenses. Immediately. If others don't understand, that's too bad. It's not the time to hide from reality and have more financial stress than you need right now.

If it's the military being unsupportive of your romantic plans, see if the two of you can plan a faster, smaller ceremony if you don't want to wait until later, and then do what's best for the two of you. You might even consider eloping and having a quick honeymoon! You can always have a party to celebrate later.

If it's a death in the family, then you and your fiancé alone know whether this is something that person would want you to go forward with. Do what your heart tells you.

 FACT

After the tragedy of September 11, many couples worried whether they should proceed with their plans to wed. One wedding planner had the following advice: Going through with the wedding can show that commitment is important to our way of life, and that it cannot be disrupted with the threats of terrorism.

When Vendors and Venues Let You Down

Perhaps one of your vendors lets you down. The bakery that was supposed to bake your wedding cake goes out of business. Your wedding dress arrives without the matching jacket for your winter wedding.

The reception site apologizes for an accidental double-booking and shows you the door.

In such a situation, the first thing you should do is check your contract. (Keep all of your agreements and contracts handy in a three-ring binder or your big wedding notebook so that if you run into a problem, you won't be frantically sifting through paperwork to find what you need.)

See what provisions you've made for deposits to be returned if delivery can't be made. Nicely but firmly threaten to contact the Better Business Bureau in your area if your vendor doesn't want to make an arrangement with you. Write letters. Make yourself a burr in the side of the individual if they think they can just say sorry and walk away from the mess.

If it's a big thing, like you've made a large deposit and now have no reception site and they refuse to come up with a compromise that is workable, contact an attorney for help. Most attorneys will tell you that they're able to resolve many differences and problems without expensive litigation and court appearances in civil actions. Their role is to work out a resolution that avoids these proceedings!

Guess Who's Coming to Dinner

So all those relatives and friends you haven't seen in a long time suddenly decided they just couldn't stay away on your happy day—but you weren't expecting them because they didn't let you know they were coming.

Don't panic. If they're expecting that you'll put them up, or pay for their hotel stay, gently but firmly tell them that you're sorry, you weren't anticipating such an expense. Offer them the information you provided the other (polite and socially responsible) guests as to where there are good accommodations and things to do. Do not, under any circumstances, break your budget to accommodate expenses for these people.

If you are having a buffet food service at your reception, you should be okay, because the caterer will have allowed for such occurrences (they are much more prepared for this kind of behavior than you are). If it's a sit-down dinner and your head count is higher than what you'd expected, ask your caterer or reception venue manager how you can work out the difference.

 QUESTION?

Worried about having too little—or too much—food?
Ask the advice of your vendor or venue. They have formulas that may be much better than any you've heard of, unless you have a lot of experience in such matters. Listen to what they suggest.

When Borrowing Is a Good Idea

Uh-oh. You've overspent. Or the money you were expecting from parents or relatives isn't forthcoming. Or that CD isn't going to be available without a penalty for early withdrawal. Or that job change happened, but you know it's temporary, and you don't want to downsize your wedding and reception or elope.

No one thinks that borrowing a lot of money or racking up lots of credit card charges to pay for a wedding is a good idea. However, if what you have is a temporary situation and you don't want to borrow much, you might think about a loan.

Keep It in the Family

Turning to family first is the best idea, unless those are the same people who caused the problem to begin with by taking back a promise of financial help. These loans don't require credit approval, interest charges, and payment dates that aren't subject to change.

Offer to sign a note for the money, with the terms for repayment stated clearly, and make certain that you intend to honor your commitment, not act like it's going to be a gift.

Turn to a Financial Institution

If you have to borrow money from a financial institution, see if you can take out a loan using your savings or CD account as collateral (which will stay in the bank or credit union until the loan is repaid, or as parts of it are repaid). If you don't have a savings account, a local bank or credit union might still approve a loan for you and/or your fiancé.

As much as possible, avoid overcharging your credit

cards. However, when all else fails, use a credit card with the lowest interest first. Remember to check out whether taking out a cash advance carries a lower interest rate, and use that first, if you can.

 ESSENTIAL

All the challenges you may face in pulling off your wedding will help you learn how to work together as a team with your fiancé. It's great practice for the Real Thing—life as a married couple—and that's worth everything, all the tears and the laughter and the heated discussions.

CHAPTER 12

How about the Budgets of Other People?

You've been thinking about the budget for your wedding and reception, and that's been quite enough work, right? Well, not exactly! While you're watching your budget, it's important to also consider the budgets of your friends and family!

The Wedding Party

The biggest way to save on expenses related to the wedding party—to you, that is—is to limit the number of attendants. While you want to have your friends who have been near and dear to you as your honor attendants, remember that by inviting them to your ceremony, they *are* with you.

Attending You Can Be Expensive

The financial side of being an attendant can be steep. Your maid of honor and bridesmaids have to pay for their dress and any needed alterations, a wrap (if needed), dress shoes, hair and makeup, any special undergarments if needed for the dress, travel expenses, and shower and wedding presents.

The groomsmen get off easier, paying for the rental of their tuxes, dress shoes, and maybe some dark socks. As you might imagine, after they say they feel honored to be a part of your wedding ceremony, your attendants start thinking about their own budgets.

The bride and groom who want to have a destination wedding where travel expenses will be steep should reveal where the ceremony will be held *before* they invite people to be in the wedding party. This way, your friends will know up front what might be involved before they get excited and agree, only to have to decline when the cold light of reality hits and they realize they can't afford it.

Informing your attendants of the wedding date as far ahead as possible is vital so that they can begin their own planning and budget making. They should be among the first told (after parents, of course!) and the first to get save-the-date cards (discussed in Chapter 7).

You Can Control Some Expenses

One of the ways you can help your maid of honor and bridesmaids save is by choosing gowns that they can wear again. For a winter wedding, think about having beautiful cashmere twin sets and satin skirts. Spring? One spring wedding featured attendants dressed in white linen blouses tied at the waist and long floral skirts. For summer—spaghetti strap dresses with pretty matching wraps. Try to find styles that don't require a lot of expensive alteration—or trips for fittings, which will take up your attendants' time.

 ALERT!

Think about treating your bridal attendants to a group session at the hairdresser's, or a facial. It's great for relaxing and getting together with the girls before you become a married woman. Many salons offer a group rate—ask if yours does!

Another area to help them save is to let them wear their own dress-appropriate shoes. Some brides want their attendants to wear dyed-to-match shoes, which can be expensive, and which aren't always a color that they can wear again. How often will you wear a pair of peach-toned satin shoes or a pair of strappy silver sandals with three-inch heels if you're a casual kind of girl?

One bride wanted all of her attendants to join her at her favorite salon on her wedding day, and the price tag was stiff for most of them—particularly the mom of the flower girl, who never envisioned that she'd have to pay $30 to have her little girl's hair combed into a simple style with a bow.

The groom can help his groomsmen save by not requiring that they rent their dress shoes from the tuxedo rental store, something the store personnel will try to emphasize they must do for a good look. The groomsmen will also appreciate wearing their own season-appropriate suits to a less formal wedding, saving on the cost of the tuxedo rental.

Inviting the wedding party to meals and special celebration dinners and making certain either that they do not pay or that the charges are very reasonable will also be appreciated by the budget-conscious. Who wants to spend a lot on airfare and the wedding attire, take time off from work and responsibilities, then find that when you get to the wedding location you must keep pulling out your wallet for every meal—especially at expensive restaurants!

Hotel and Travel Accommodations

It's almost certain that at least a few of your guests will

be traveling to the wedding from out of town. It's up to you to decide whether you will be paying for their travel and accommodations. Travel expenses may include not only the airfare and hotel, but also the taxi or shuttle charges.

Even if you choose not to pay for all of their expenses, you still need to provide them with information and options. The bride and groom can arrange for special hotel or motel rates for their wedding party (especially if they are using that hotel for their reception). Make certain the wedding party and other guests know they must ask for the special rate by requesting the "Smith wedding party rate."

 FACT

It's great if you can accommodate your wedding party attendants at your home or with your family or local friends—as long as the accommodations are reasonable.

Time Is Everything

The bride and groom can save their wedding party a lot of money by setting the date early so that the best airfare and hotel rates can be arranged. Remember the advice that you can save on your wedding by having it at a time and date that aren't the most popular—like on a Friday, for instance, instead of the more popular Saturday? Well, scheduling weddings during certain times of the year might be hard on your guests' wallets, too.

One bride was so caught up with planning for her wedding that she forgot all about the big balloon festival that took place in her town the week she planned to wed. Her mother, who lived out of town, called to book a room, found out there was nothing available, and quickly alerted her daughter. The bride decided she didn't want to change the date and even thought it would be great to let her guests know that they could participate in the festival as a side activity to the wedding.

She found some creative ways to put up her guests, asking friends and family if they'd mind doing this, and locating hotels and motels that weren't as well known to visitors.

Check with your local chamber of commerce or visitor's bureau to see if there are any big events scheduled during the week of your wedding. This will ensure that your guests don't have a difficult time finding rooms, or end up paying dramatically marked-up rates.

If you're having your reception in a hotel, talk to the site coordinator about a special price for rooms for your wedding guests. Be aware that while this may be a wonderful location for your reception, the rooms might be pricey for some of your guests, especially if it's peak season for some kind of event or vacation during the week of your wedding. Have a few alternate choices you can offer those who need information on a place to stay. If you haven't visited these hotels or motels, ask your friends or coworkers about them so you can save time over checking them out personally.

Don't be in airfare denial—sometimes the longer you wait, the steeper the price. Airfares might zoom astronomically during certain times of the year—or seats might be totally unavailable. Remind guests to tie down those airline reservations. Who needs to pay lots extra because they waited to make reservations and the NBA playoffs come to your city the week of your wedding!

 ALERT!

Don't forget that a travel agent may be a very good resource for you and your guests. Also, be sure to inquire about discounts if you have an American Automobile Association (AAA) membership or other membership that offers travelers discounts.

Your consideration of your guests with some easily looked-up names and numbers of hotel and motel, airline, and transportation companies will be a great money- and time-saving service to your guests, who are coming to help you celebrate your special day!

Planning for Out-of-Town Guests

Many people take vacation days or a long weekend to attend a wedding, so they'll want some downtime while they're in town. You can't be with them every minute, and they probably wouldn't want you to be anyway, so giving them some suggestions for that downtime might be welcome.

If you check with your local chamber of commerce or tourist bureau, you'll have some ideas of special events you can mention to your out-of-town guests. Typing up a quick list of spots for them to think about visiting is a nice touch. You can include this in an informal note, or post it on your wedding Web site.

One couple tucked such a list into a little gift bag with a few fancy snack items and asked the hotel where their guests were staying to pass them out when they checked in. Another couple listed the top ten things to do while visiting, and provided links on their Web site for convenience.

Gift Registries for All Budgets

We all know that you don't invite people to your wedding just to get a present. And while most people would love to get you the biggest and best present ever because they're so happy for you, unfortunately their budgets just won't allow it! How can you and your fiancé help them choose just the right wedding present?

Register for Practical Gifts

First, look at what you really need. Do you and your fiancé have a lot of household items? Or are you just starting out? What do you truly need? It's tempting to register for those decorating-type items that you want so much, but if you have four rather threadbare towels between you, it's time to reconsider!

Some of the basic items you'll need are tableware, flatware, cookware, glassware, small kitchen appliances, and linens for bath and bed. Unless you have a practical everyday set of dishes or china, you'll want to put that down as an item in your registry, with flatware that looks good with it. Make certain that you specify how many place settings—you probably won't need setting for a dozen, and your guests won't be happy if they hear that you've returned the ones they bought.

Where should you register? If most of your guests live in the same city or town, it might be okay to use one or two stores as your registries. But if some of your guests live out of town, then using nationwide registries will help save them time and money.

 ALERT!

It might seem that the way to save money is to include your registry information on your wedding invitation, but wedding etiquette experts advise couples not to do it.

WeddingChannel.com is a one-stop registry that includes big department stores such as Neiman Marcus, Burdines, Gump's, and similar stores. Do you love Pottery Barn and Bed, Bath, and Beyond? They have Web sites your guests can access if they don't have those stores in their hometowns, or don't have the time to visit. With a click of their mouse, they can see what you've registered for and order it. If they're uncomfortable with ordering over the Internet, there are toll-free numbers listed for the customers' convenience.

Gifts Aren't Really the Point Anyway

If you have your household fairly well established or for some other reason don't want or need your guests to buy items for it, let them know. You could suggest alternatives, simply say "no gifts please," or ask that they donate to their favorite charity. They'll be happy that you've saved them the money and time spent shopping. If they've taken you up on your suggestion that they donate to a charity of their choice, not only will someone in need benefit, but your guest(s) will likely get a tax deduction as well.

Gift Alternatives—Make It for Me

If your guest is particularly skilled at making something you've always admired, such as crafts or a quilt or something similar, don't be afraid to ask if you could have one of those items for your wedding present because you'd treasure it much more than a store-bought gift.

Perhaps you have a photographer in your family or on your guest list. While an entire wedding package might be a bit much to ask for, perhaps you could request an engagement portrait or something similar.

Chances are, your photographer family member or guest might be flattered enough to do your entire wedding and reception. It pays to ask.

If a family member or guest is a whiz at making fancy cakes and you feel they'd do a good job for you (no amateurs on this important day!), tell them how much you would love for them to make your cake. While there may be a large time investment for the baker (if it's a big or heavily decorated cake), the ingredients are not expensive, and it's such a savings for the wedding couple!

 ESSENTIAL

> If your family member or guest is willing to make a cake as his or her present to you, it needn't be a daylong job. Your "gift" baker can make a simple layered, frosted cake and then you can add fresh or silk flowers or a special cake topper at the reception site.

Other possibilities for handmade gifts that can save your guests money—and show them how much you appreciate their handiwork—are fancy favors for the reception tables. (Some favor ideas are discussed in Chapter 10.)

With all the talk of wedding registries and store-bought gifts, perhaps your guests are too shy to think about offering something they've made. Tell them their handmade gift would be very special to you, worth so much more than any expensive gift they could buy!

Personalized Wedding Web Sites

Have you seen the Web sites some couples are creating about their weddings? They even have a catchy name: "wedsites."

A wedsite may contain a variety of information about the upcoming wedding: a story of how the couple met, some photos, directions to the wedding site, links to local attractions and events, and so on. Some of these Web sites are very creative—sometimes the couples share funny stories about each other, or their visions of their future together; some may feature a time clock to show how many days, hours, minutes, and seconds are left until the Big Event.

Visitors to the wedsite can RSVP there, let the bride and groom know what entrée they want at the reception meal, advise them of any special needs, find out what hotel the wedding party has a group rate at, and more. And you'll avoid all those long-distance calls and repeating the same information to all of your guests individually.

And think of the money saved on sending everyone pictures of the wedding and the honeymoon! Digital pictures can be downloaded to your Web site almost immediately. You could even post a streaming video of your wedding, so that friends and family who had to miss the wedding can see what happened.

QUESTION?

> **Is a wedding Web site a good idea for me?**
> If you and your fiancé are outgoing and want
> to share this wonderful time with others, yes.
> If one or both of you is uncomfortable with
> the idea of sharing personal information,
> maybe not. Of course, you can limit the
> amount of information you share—omitting
> the location of the wedding ceremony, for
> instance, or protecting some information on
> your site with a password.

How Much Do You Spend to Save?

Prices for hosting your Web site will vary widely, from "free" to more than a hundred dollars a month. "Free" can mean that the fee is small because there will be advertising on the site—advertising you may not care for! Some sites require you to be a techie to set them up. Others are slick, easily assembled packages that require little from you beyond typing in some information and e-mailing pictures.

Before opting to go with a free or low-cost site, use these questions to decide whether it's a good idea for you:

1. Will there be advertising on our site?
2. What kind of design options do we get?
3. When my site visitors RSVP, will their e-mail addresses be collected?

4. Can we set up links to other sites?
5. Are there interactive features such as maps or message boards?
6. How much is this going to cost? What kind of contract do we have to sign?

Companies that charge for helping you create a wedding Web site abound on the Internet. A search on Yahoo revealed a number, including the following:

  ✎ *www.loveyourweddingsite.com*
  ✎ *www.virtuallymarried.com*
  ✎ *www.ourperfectday.com*

A couple of sites that offer free Web sites are The Knot (✎*www.theknot.com*) and iVillage (✎*www.ivillage.com*).

CHAPTER 13

Pre-wedding Celebrations

The fun of getting married isn't limited to your wedding day. From engagement parties and wedding showers to bachelor/bachelorette parties and rehearsal dinners, you'll have plenty of opportunities to celebrate—and plenty of expenses to budget.

The Engagement Party

A great way to save money on your wedding and reception lies in having a party—yes, a party! Wherever you decide to hold your wedding, there will likely be friends and family who won't be able to travel there. Perhaps you and your spouse don't come from the same hometown. If, for instance, you are getting married in your hometown, why not have an engagement party near his parents' home, so that his friends and relatives can attend.

An engagement party is also a good way to include friends and associates in your personal happiness without feeling you must invite them to an expensive (and often intimate) wedding and reception—and they don't have to buy a present for you, either! More people are choosing to have a small, intimate ceremony these days. Having an engagement party lets a much wider circle of friends, associates, and extended family share the happiness.

Another Party?

How can having a party—and spending money—help you save money? Simple! Have you heard the rumor that reception sites and caterers sometimes mark up the amount they charge the minute they hear wedding bells? Well, whether this is true or not, engagement parties often don't come with the expense of a wedding reception.

ESSENTIAL

Combining an engagement party with a holiday celebration will save you time and money. The decorations will serve both occasions, and the holiday just puts everyone in a celebratory mood.

The food can be simpler, the cake less elaborate (that is, if you want a cake), there are no worries about flowers or favors, and—well, you get the drift!

Better yet is the fact that most of the time, the event can take place in the home of the bride or groom or that of their families. In summertime, you could have a barbecue out on the patio, a buffet beside the pool, a cookout at an area park by a river or lake—these are all possible places to tell everyone the happy news about your engagement. In cold-weather months, you'll move indoors for a fun get-together at a clubhouse, a community center, or a fraternal hall.

Making the Food Without Stressing Out

Save money by making much of the food yourself, and save time and stress by keeping the menu simple and using shortcuts. Like barbecuing? Buy chicken when it's on sale at the grocery store, and stash it away in the freezer. Brush on a homemade or bottled barbecue sauce and serve corn on the cob and pasta salad. Dessert? Serve apple pie or order a cake filled with ice cream and decorated with an icing picture of the happy couple.

For that buffet by the pool, make it Italian. Serve those big family-size frozen lasagnas. Pop them out of the aluminum pans while they're still frozen, put them in your own casserole dishes, and bake—and no one will know the difference! Add an antipasto platter of olives, peppers, Italian ham and cheeses, marinated artichokes, mushrooms, and so on. Crusty bread or rolls and cannoli from your local Italian bakery complete this easy-on-the-hosts meal.

 FACT

If you don't cook much or you find an anxiety attack coming on at the thought of computing how much of the ingredients you'll have to buy to feed your guests, simply visit *www.allrecipes.com*. The recipes include a handy feature that will adjust the recipe and tell you exactly how much of each food to buy!

The Wedding Shower

Sometimes friends and family want to give the bride a shower, but that means additional expenses for those people who already have to worry about all the expenses associated with attending (and perhaps participating in) your wedding.

If the shower is not a surprise, you can let your

friends and relatives know that you want them to keep it simple, "for the sake of everyone's budget." Emphasize that the shower is an opportunity for making great memories and female bonding, which is far more important to you than expensive gifts or a fancy party.

Basket Showers

Some great inexpensive shower gifts can start with a basket shower. Start by decorating the food table with baskets of crudités and dips, chips, pretzels, and so on, and then put napkins and silverware in other baskets. Tuck casserole baking dishes into baskets at serving time, and serve the breads and rolls in a napkin-lined basket.

Each guest decides what theme their gift basket will be—for the kitchen, bath, master bedroom, home office, leisure-time activity, and so on. The kitchen basket can be lined with a pretty kitchen towel and filled with cooking utensils, pot holders, recipe cards, and so on, all bought at the big discount store for super savings (stay away from those houseware stores at the mall—they're expensive). A basket for the bathroom might contain some pretty hand towels, fancy soaps, some aromatherapy candles, and other similar items. For the master bedroom, how about those little nightlights for reading while your significant other is sleeping, scented sachets for the clothing drawers, or some satin padded hangers for the closet.

Or try a "first night at home" basket—ready-made pasta, a jar of good-quality sauce, a package of amaretto cookies, cappuccino mix, perhaps a bottle of wine, all wrapped in a checked cloth. You get the idea. When a few of the above items are presented in a basket available in the craft section of your local discount store, you've got a great gift for real savings.

 QUESTION?

What about giving money?
Some guests do give a check or a gift certificate as a wedding shower gift, and that's certainly perfectly acceptable—sometimes even preferred. Maybe you want to drop a hint that you could use that money to pay for wedding or honeymoon expenses.

Bachelor and Bachelorette Parties

Having a bachelor party is a tradition, but women have also joined in on the fun by having a bachelorette party these days to celebrate and mourn the bride-to-be's last days as a single woman. Sometimes, these parties can get a little racy; sometimes, they're just a chance to have some fun and relax with your best friends before the wedding.

Whatever the type of party, there are many ways to have a great celebration without spending a lot of money. Traditionally, the maid or matron of honor gives the bride her party, and the groom's best man gives his. However, it's great if several people take on the planning.

It's best to plan these parties at least several days before the wedding; they can take place up to a month before the big day—you don't want the bride and groom to show up bleary-eyed at their own wedding!

Some Fun Ideas

Great budget-saving ideas for a bachelorette party include a pajama party at someone's home. Break out a bottle or two of champagne, rent some "chick flicks," and pretend you're all at the spa with a basket of pampering goodies like facials and manicure items. Or, hire a belly dancer to come teach all of you to do the sensuous dance, and offer plenty of Middle Eastern finger food. Gifts? Something inexpensive—gag gifts are even better!

Guy parties? How about the kind of "man's man" party there's never enough time to hold? Have a poker night complete with cigars and plenty of subs, potato chips, and beer. Or go paintballing, camping, fishing, or some other sport you all enjoy. Has the groom ever been skydiving? Don't think pushing him out of a plane is a good idea just a week or two before his wedding. Check and see if there is a virtual skydiving facility near you. Everyone can get all the thrill of the jump with none of the worry about a broken ankle!

Bachelor and bachelorette parties can get expensive if done "out on the town," where there is less control over the amount of alcoholic drinks ordered, which costs everyone too much money. Have your party at home, where you can be comfortable, be as loud as you want, and save money, too!

The Rehearsal Dinner

First of all, you should remember this: A rehearsal dinner is not a reception! After all, you've spent a lot of time and money on the reception the next day, and you want that occasion to be the standout of the wedding-related festivities. Then, too, it's a last time for your family and wedding party (which includes those so-very-close friends) to gather together on the eve of the Big Day.

More couples are choosing to have their rehearsal dinners at the home of their parents or a close relative. It can be a challenge to get everyone together for the rehearsal, and you don't want to feel pressured to be on time for your restaurant reservation.

 QUESTION?

Who comes to a rehearsal dinner?
Everyone who's invited to the rehearsal, of course. That means those in the wedding party and their significant others, the parents of the bride and groom, the minister and spouse, close friends, and relatives (especially out-of-town ones).

When a Rehearsal Dinner Isn't a Dinner

Although it's called a rehearsal dinner, it doesn't have to be a *dinner*. If you're having the rehearsal earlier in the day, make it a lunch or afternoon event. Sometimes, if the church or synagogue or other ceremony site isn't available earlier, the rehearsal will be done just before the wedding, so you could hold the rehearsal "dinner" whenever you choose, the day or two before.

Making It Easy on the Hosts

Because the people who are at the rehearsal are the ones playing host, you don't want them stressing over how they're going to get the food ready. They shouldn't be rushing off to put things on the table when they need to hear what to do on the wedding day—or worse yet, keeping everyone waiting when they're probably starving!

Some Menu Ideas

This is the afternoon or evening when you want things super-easy, not needing a lot of heating or fussing, and yet you don't want to break the budget by having to pay a lot for prepared food. Decide what type of mood you want to set; your choice should be based on your tastes, budget, and the expected crowd. You can adjust the menu from very casual to very elegant, depending on how much time and money you want to spend. You could even do something like dessert and coffee if that is what you want to do instead of a meal.

Want spring or summertime casual and inexpensive? Set out a buffet of sliced meats and cheeses from the deli with an assortment of breads and rolls, several cold salads, lots of pickles and olives, and condiments. Add several types of fancy ice creams and sherbets for a cool finish to the meal.

Want something more elegant? Try making several fancy entrées or casserole-type dishes, like a chicken-asparagus gratin or beef burgundy, freeze them, then thaw in the refrigerator the day of the rehearsal. When you arrive home, serve your guests some simple appetizers or a tossed salad with several types of dressing while the casseroles heat. If there is a French or Italian bakery in your area, fancy bakery cookies are a good choice for a dessert that's elegant but budget-conscious.

 ALERT!

A buffet is easier on the hosts than a more formal sit-down dinner, but caterers and other food professionals will tell you that people will eat more food when they serve themselves from a buffet. Be sure to plan for this if you want to have a buffet!

Let Them Cook!

Does it still sound like more work than you want? Then have the rehearsal meal at a restaurant, or have it catered. It's totally up to you and your budget!

It's best to work out a set menu if you're having a meal in a restaurant, because it'll save on the price and lessen aggravation. No one wants to get mad at Uncle Bert because he orders lobster when everyone else is being careful of your budget.

Then, too, you want everyone served at about the

same time, and that's hard if there are too many menu selections to cook. A set menu doesn't mean that you have only one entrée—it just means that you offer two or three entrée choices, not let every guest decide what they want. This set menu also includes certain things that have been prearranged, such as a salad, entrée, dessert, and nonalcoholic beverage.

Ask the restaurant if they have some sample set menus that have worked for other events, and talk with them about alcohol if you want it served. If you haven't eaten at that particular restaurant before, be sure to stop by and sample the food.

QUESTION?

> **Who pays for the rehearsal dinner?**
> In the past, the groom's family played host for the rehearsal dinner. Today, it's totally up to you to decide who pays.

Or, you can have your rehearsal meal prepared by the caterer you have hired for your wedding reception meal. The advantages are obvious: You've already checked out this person or company and feel good about their service and food, and you may be able to work out a better price if they see they can get more business from you. Just make sure that the meal served for the rehearsal is sufficiently different from that of the reception so that guests don't feel they're having the same thing twice.

Potluck and Memories

If you're part of a family that loves to cook, a potluck dinner might be a wonderful idea for your rehearsal dinner. Take this opportunity to connect with your families' culinary heritage.

Have one person keep a list of who's bringing what so you don't end up with too many desserts or entrées, and let the fun begin! Ask those bringing the dishes to write out the recipe and make enough photocopies for sharing. A great present for the new couple would be an album or three-ring notebook filled with these treasured family recipes.

Pictures of family members cooking their specialties and serving them at the rehearsal dinner would be a wonderful addition to the album. One person in the family could make this their project and have an inexpensive but so very thoughtful wedding gift for the couple!

The types of food brought to a potluck are as diverse as the people who make up your big family of friends and relatives. Selections can be as simple and inexpensive as Aunt Gertrude's stuffed cabbage rolls to the more complicated and elegant crêpes with several different fillings that Cousin Francine brings.

Let Us Entertain You

Whatever type of party you're involved in, chances are there'll be entertainment. You just can't get a group of people together for a happy occasion and not have some fun.

ESSENTIAL

One family found a free way to entertain the family at the rehearsal dinner. They set up equipment to play old home movies of the bride and groom as kids, and the two families bonded while watching their "babies" grow up into the adults about to be married.

Music Makes It Special

It's good to have some appropriate music playing in the background of your parties and celebrations, but there is no need to go to extra expense for this. Ask friends and family to loan you CDs and tapes, and if there are any performers or "hams" in your group, let them entertain you!

CHAPTER 14

The Honeymoon of Your Dreams

Imagine—the vacation of your dreams, just the two of you. It's your honeymoon, the time you'll get to start a new life together as husband and wife. You've saved as much as you could, and planned every aspect carefully, so now the two of you should have the honeymoon of your dreams. Where will you go? What will you do?

What Are You Dreaming Of?

When you took the quiz at the beginning of the book, how alike were you? Did you agree on most aspects of your wedding? What about your honeymoon? Were your tastes similar, or did one of you dream of flying away to an island paradise and the other want to do a driving tour of several states and stop here and there at charming little bed-and-breakfasts? What kind of honeymoon will please you both?

Sit down together one evening and do nothing but think about that honeymoon. If the two of you have high-stress jobs, and you add in the stress of planning your wedding and reception, you may want peace and relaxation. Does the idea of sitting on a sunny beach, sipping margaritas, and thinking about absolutely nothing appeal to you? Or are you full of energy and love to sightsee and shop in a big city?

 FACT

> The top honeymoon destinations in the Caribbean are Jamaica, the Bahamas, Mexico, and St. Lucia. Hawaii, Las Vegas, New York, and San Francisco are sites honeymooners most often prefer if they want a city venue.

The Possibilities Are Endless

Do you both love cold-weather sports like skiing? Many ski lodges offer instruction if one or both of you has never skied. Then there are those long winter nights in front of a blazing fire and cozying up in a big feather bed. Is your idea of luxury a cabin in the mountains, with the only sound the wind in the trees at night and the only light the stars overhead?

What about a cruise? It's truly the getaway of getaways. You relax on deck, have all the amenities of a luxury hotel with swimming pools, restaurants, lounges, planned activities you're free to enjoy or not, shops, hair salons—you name it—and then you're docking at an island for sightseeing or snorkeling or whatever you like.

Some places are just naturally romantic and lend themselves to a honeymoon. But remember that it's the two of you who create the romance. The location and the price have nothing to do with it!

What's Your Honeymoon Budget?

What kind of budget do you have for your honeymoon? Remember how the wedding and reception budgets were termed modest, moderate, and luxurious (splurge)? Well, think of your honeymoon budget the same way.

A Modest Budget

If you are on a modest budget, try to compromise what you want with what you can afford. For example, if you'd love to go to a tropical island but don't have the budget, what about visiting Florida (or another coastline state) and staying in one of the smaller beach towns?

Don't think of it as less than what you wanted. Think of the hassles you'll save yourself—passports aren't necessary! When you're sitting on a sandy beach, a mai tai in your hand, you may feel like you've found just the island paradise for your budget.

Learn to Bargain

Most Americans aren't used to bargaining, except maybe when they go car-shopping. However, there is no reason for you not to ask questions and seek a better deal. Dustin, our college graduate on a modest wedding budget, calculated what a bed-and-breakfast in a nearby state charged and figured that he and Amanda could afford five days. But they wanted to stay a week. So, Dustin called the bed-and-breakfast and explained his problem. And guess what? "They did it!" he enthused. "They never would have if I hadn't told them about the honeymoon, and if I hadn't *asked*! It really helped us since we are students on a budget!"

A Moderate or Splurge Budget

If you're like Tammie and Matt and family is paying for much of your wedding, you may have a bit more to spend for your honeymoon. "We're going for one of those all-inclusive package deals in the Bahamas," said Tammie. "We found some great deals in the back of a bridal magazine, looked into it, and it's just what we wanted. It'll help stretch our budget for the honeymoon."

Stretch even the most luxurious budget, and get the most for your money by not insisting on having the best room in the best place in your location. After all, you'll be out and about so much, you might not care that you don't have the most deluxe accommodations. Reserve a portion of your budget for that unexpected special restaurant you spot or a gift you just can't resist in a little boutique you discover. Remember to budget a portion for tips and unexpected expenses.

 ESSENTIAL

Check visitors bureaus and tourist organizations for lists of hotels and motels, as well as local attractions and special deals and discount coupons. Compare the price of a rental condo, popular in some areas, with other types of accommodations.

Timing Is Everything

Try not to plan a honeymoon for a location at its peak season. Do you know when that peak season is for the location you'd like? Investigate. The last thing you want is to go someplace that turns out to be crowded and overpriced. That's not the honeymoon you've been dreaming of.

For example, many people take vacations in the summer, when their work schedules slow or their children are out of school. Some of these people rush to Florida for their vacations. People in Florida will tell you that they themselves don't think it's the best season for doing a lot of things the tourists do—it's too hot! Floridians tend to stay indoors a lot in the summer. Their off-season is a better time to see Florida, when it's not 105 degrees outside and you don't have to stand in line with many fellow tourists.

 QUESTION?

How do I find out the peak season for a travel venue?
Just ask! Call the travel venue or visit their Web site. They're eager to fill those rooms during the nonpeak season and will be happy to offer the information. Or call or visit a travel agent.

Speaking of time, just how much time can you budget for a honeymoon? Not every couple can take two weeks. "Things are really busy around the time we're getting married, so we're taking just a week," said JoEllen. "We've promised ourselves two weeks in Hawaii later this year."

Planning Ahead for Great Bargains

The fact that you are usually planning your wedding and reception six to twelve months ahead of your wedding date will help you because you have enough lead time to do some honeymoon investigation. The farther ahead you make those airline or train reservations and book that room, the more you'll save. With this much time to plan ahead, you can do some surfing on the Internet and get great ideas as well as great prices.

Be Aware

Does a particular travel deal sound too good to be true? Well, guess what—it probably is! There is perhaps no better time to remind you to put everything on a credit card and get everything in writing than when you make travel arrangements. No one needs to have a bad experience at such an important time as their honeymoon. It just sours everything to find that you've been gypped.

Be wary of any travel deal that is too aggressively marketed by a telemarketer or someone who represents him- or herself as a travel professional. If urgency is stressed, it's probably a scam. Take the time to check things out with the Better Business Bureau or an accredited travel agent.

Know the Add-Ons

A great room rate might not seem so great if you find that there are lots of little charges you hadn't expected. For instance, is there a local tourist-type surcharge on the rooms? What about tax? Even though everyone in the area may have to add those things on, it's important to get the total figure so as to avoid price shock later.

Room service is such a great feature—no need to go out when you don't want to, and it's understood that honeymooners usually don't want to the first day or two.

But $6 for a glass of tomato juice with breakfast? And $3 for a bottle of water? If you're watching your budget, you'll want to be very careful to use room service and the little minibar in the rooms judiciously.

 ESSENTIAL

Make sure your travel agent is a member of a recognized professional organization such as the American Society of Travel Agents ✆(703/739-8739) or the National Tour Association ✆(606/226-4444) or U.S. Tour Operators Association ✆(212/599-6599).

Ten Ways to Save

Here are ten ideas to keep in mind as you plan for your honeymoon. Some of this advice appeared elsewhere in the book, but it applies specifically to your honeymoon planning:

1. Time your honeymoon for the site's best rates. Call a hotel directly, because a hotel chain toll-free-number operator might not know special deals relevant to the particular hotel you're interested in. Also, visit *www.hotelcoupons.com*, *www.hoteldiscounts.com*, or another Web site that offers similar service to get information about special deals.
2. Leave for the honeymoon during your air carrier's best rate time (usually midweek).

FACT

Disney World and Disneyland are popular sites with honeymooners because there are so many fun things to do and they offer so many different price categories. Check out ✍ *www.waltdisney world.com* or ✍ *www.disneyland.com*. Also take a look at ✍ *www.amusementpark.com* for deals on amusement parks around the country.

3. Don't eat all your meals in a restaurant during your honeymoon. Cook some, and make picnic breakfasts and lunches to take to the park or the beach.
4. The farther away the location, the more expensive—staying within a few hundred miles will save you airfare or gas, if you're traveling by car.
5. Consider a package deal if it works for you.
6. Use one credit card to charge your purchases for your wedding and rack up frequent flier miles for your honeymoon airfare.
7. Check out bridal magazine honeymoon sections, or visit ✍ *www.theknot.com* for information on booking great honeymoon deals.
8. Two words: *honeymoon registry*. Guests can contribute to it instead of buying you a present for, say, the kitchen or bath.
9. Don't automatically choose the cheapest price for anything—room, airfare, whatever—or you could

chance making an expensive mistake. Examine
what it includes very carefully.

10. There *is* such a thing as a "shoulder season"—that
means times in between peak and nonpeak seasons, when you get a price break not as good as
nonpeak, but still better than peak.

 FACT

Disney World and Disneyland are popular sites
with honeymooners because there are so many
fun things to do and they offer so many different
price categories. Check out ✍*www.waltdisney
world.com* or ✍*www.disneyland.com*. Also take
a look at ✍*www.amusementpark.com* for deals
on amusement parks around the country.

When Things Go Wrong

So you've planned and you've researched and you've
picked your destination, bought the tickets, and made all
the arrangements—and you are there. So what happens
if you are not happy with what you see?

No Room at the Inn?

What if you arrive at your honeymoon hotel and
nothing is as it was promised? How can you keep your
dream honeymoon from becoming a nightmare? First,
calmly explain to the check-in clerk what you were
promised, and pull out that confirmation of your

reservation with a price quote and any other material. Ask for an adjustment. If that doesn't work, ask to speak to a supervisor or manager. Explain that you are here on your honeymoon and you know that the hotel doesn't want to disappoint you. Ask that the matter be corrected, and if there is some compelling reason why it cannot be—something went wrong with the reservation process, too many guests stayed over that shouldn't have—whatever!—ask that the hotel make some kind of arrangement for you.

If you still can't get satisfaction, you may want to excuse yourself for a moment and go to a telephone and call around to see if you can find a better accommodation. If your site was overbooked, chances are it's happening all around that area. If not, you may want to go elsewhere and fight with the first hotel once you get home.

Food Fights

If you're in a restaurant and your meal arrives cold, badly prepared, or is simply not what you ordered, calmly ask for it to be taken back and redone. Most people will not do this, not wanting to cause a fuss, but there is a big difference between causing a scene and being a customer who is reasonably unsatisfied and is asking for better food or service.

Again, ask to speak to the supervisor or manager if you don't get results. Now, you can't leave the restaurant without paying—you might get arrested! So if the restaurant is not willing to make good, again, pay with your credit card and later dispute the charge when you get home.

Hey, It Rained—Pay Up!

What if you have to cancel your honeymoon—or cut it short—because a hurricane is heading toward your island paradise? This is the time to have you reconsider wedding insurance (see Chapter 10). Your policy will cover any honeymoon disasters. Check out companies offering wedding insurance on the Internet, or call your insurance agent.

Even if you don't want to invest in a wedding insurance policy, look into travel insurance offered by the vendors you are dealing with, such as the cruise line, the car rental agency, and so on. Travel agents are also good advisors on how to protect yourself from losing money due to unforeseen circumstances while traveling.

 QUESTION?

Think you've heard the best honeymoon disaster story?
Take a look at a contest Thrifty Car Rental sponsors on its Web site, *www.thrifty.com/honeymoon.* The winner receives a new trip, cash award, a car rental, and a chance to have a better time next time!

Accent the Positive

Few things are perfect. When all is said and done, how you and your new spouse react to the ups and downs of any problem you encounter during your honeymoon is important. Try to take it in stride and not overreact. After all, few disasters on any modern-day honeymoon will equal what more than a dozen honeymooning couples faced when the Titanic went down.

Remember, your honeymoon may be the first trip you'll take together, but it won't be your last. Don't try to do everything and exhaust not only your budget, but your energies and good humor. If you love where you've gone on a honeymoon, promise each other that you'll return. The happiest married couples make time and save money for those special trips together to renew their relationship on a regular basis.

CHAPTER 15
Creative Budget Ideas

There are so many other great ideas to save money on your wedding that a special chapter was needed to let you know all about them. So here it is, a compendium, a potpourri, a veritable goody basket of ideas to use!

The Thrill of the Hunt

"I think I had a real change of attitude about budgets and shopping for bargains after I went shopping with my favorite aunt the other day," a friend named Bridget said recently. "She has the money to buy what she wants, but I noticed that she went for the sale racks and bargain-shopped instead of paying full price. 'It's the thrill of the hunt,' she told me. 'If I find something I want at a bargain price, I've won, I've beaten the system.' I like that attitude. If I find ways to pay for something under my budgeted figure, I can then have that extra money for something really special that I want, or just bank the money and come out ahead for the honeymoon."

Become a Bargain Hunter

One woman who has some stunning art in her home shops at art festivals on Sunday afternoons, when the artists don't want to be packing up their work and taking it home. A flea-market bargain shopper uses the same philosophy and has bagged many items for less.

How can this help you with making your wedding purchases? Since brides are encouraged to plan their weddings a year or more ahead, figure out what season will apply to your wedding purchases, then wait for the end-of-season sale. The big bridal stores run sales several times a year; check them out, but be sure that it's a true sale, that tags haven't been marked up just to look like one.

Look at the racks of discontinued dresses—"last season's dresses." Remember that just because the manufacturer has decided to go in a different direction doesn't mean that what you see is unfashionable. When the trend turned to those huge, puffy sleeves on wedding dresses years ago, there were plenty of brides who were delighted to look in "last year's" designs on the bargain rack.

 FACT

> You can save hundreds—or even thousands—of dollars if you're willing not to believe that you must have the latest styles you see in the fashion magazines. Besides, a good wedding dress design should be timeless—it shouldn't be so trendy that it's only "in" this year, and will be "out" next year.

The Fine Art of Negotiating

Negotiating is all about options—about you deciding what you want, what you want to pay for what you want, and what you want to do if you don't get what you want.

It's very simple: Negotiating is about personal power and self-control, and about keeping your ultimate goal in mind—saving on everything that you can so that you have the money for the special things you desire.

Don't Be Afraid to Ask

What many people don't realize is that very often, there are shopkeepers and vendors willing to negotiate the price. Veteran shoppers of antique fairs, flea markets, and other places where bargains abound will tell you that those shopkeepers and vendors feel very vulnerable when the flow of customers slows and their merchandise isn't moving.

Part of the skill of a negotiator lies in asking. You'll never know what you can get until you ask. Basically, there are two possible answers—yes and no. We've all dealt with rejection, and lived through it, so if you're told that you can't have what you're negotiating for, you won't suffer a humiliating fate or die. Politely thank the vendor and move on.

The Negotiating Technique

Here is a simple way to negotiate. Approach the shopkeeper or vendor when he or she is not hassled by too many people at once. If you notice that the shopkeeper you are trying to approach just had an unpleasant conversation with a customer before you, use this to your advantage by smiling sympathetically and being extra courteous in your request.

Explain your situation—for example, that there is a stain on a dress you are interested in buying, that you would like to get a discount on this damaged product. If it's an item that is dangerously out-of-season, like a swimsuit at the end of the summer or a summer wedding gown that is still on the rack long past the time a bride could wear it without shivering, then you should mention that fact. Have an idea in your head of how much you would like to see the item discounted. If the shopkeeper or vendor agrees, you've just saved yourself some money.

 ESSENTIAL

> If you're not sure if you can do it, practice negotiating with a friend until you feel more confident. It's a skill that will come in handy when you want something like a raise at work or a better deal on a significant purchase like a home or a car.

If you receive a figure that doesn't seem like a bargain, express regret and say what you were hoping the price would be, because it will take X amount of time and money to make this item something that you can use. If the item is expensive, be sure to mention that you are spending a lot of money. Also, if you shop in the store or other retail location frequently, let the salesperson know.

If you don't get what you want a second time, ask *very* politely if the salesperson can approach the store manager to see if a price adjustment could be made. Often, salespeople don't have the authority to make a price change. If there is not an adjustment at this point, politely express regret, shake your head, and say that you're sorry, you just won't be able to take it. Turn and prepare to return the item to the rack or shelf or whatever. If you're with someone, say you guess you're just going to have to look elsewhere, so you'd both better be leaving now.

See what happens when you do this—you may well hear a "Wait, let me see what I can do" called after you. Be gracious as they make another offer and see if you are happy with that. If not, decide whether you want the item or want to continue shopping.

It's just that easy to negotiate. Once you've tried the technique and had success, you will become a convert and not want to pay full price again. Remember, it's not a question of whether you *can* spend the money. It's that you don't want to—you want to spend the money you save on something else.

 FACT

At *www.celebrityweddingsonline.com,* you can take a peek at the vows favorite celebrities used on their important day (actually, since most of them marry often, it should be days, right?). Choose the vows used by Kurt Cobain and Courtney Love, members of The Beatles, Julia Roberts, and more.

Then There's Bartering

Is there some skill or product that you have that you can offer to barter—in other words, trade—for something you want? Bartering is, simply put, exchanging things rather than paying for them with money. I have something you want; you have something I want; we exchange those things instead of paying each other. Why is this good? Neither of us might have the money to pay for those things we want, but we have things we can trade for them. It's simple!

A Lesson in Bartering

A friend whose father was an artist remembers a time a neighbor approached him and said how much he liked a painting and wished he could afford to buy it. The artist appreciated the man's enthusiasm for the painting and mentioned that he thought the man was a really talented woodworker—he'd seen a coffee table that the man made.

They looked at each other for a long moment, obviously thinking, and then the artist offered to trade the woodworker the painting in return for the coffee table. They both walked away happy. That's a great example of bartering.

Could you walk into a bridal store and offer to barter with the saleswoman for a gown? Maybe not. But think about what goods and services you need, and think about whether there is the possibility of bartering something that might benefit the other person and save you money.

How Can You Use Bartering?

You might be experienced with creating Web sites and can offer to create one in exchange for something that the shopkeeper or vendor has to offer. Perhaps the venue that will be hosting your reception looks like it needs some service like painting or decorating, which you or your fiancé do. Not only might you save money on goods and services for your wedding, you might get some nice publicity or future business from the bartering opportunity.

Think about whether there is an opportunity and explore it mentally before you approach the other person so that you will be prepared to negotiate the barter. Use the same technique as for negotiating—except that instead of asking for a discount, you are offering to trade a service—or, if a complete swap of the item or service isn't possible, you *can* ask for a barter with some cash still exchanging hands. If you have a business card, you can always leave it with the shopkeeper or vendor so that they can think about your offer.

One Example of Bartering

"I'm part-owner of a local print shop, and when I walked into the small hotel where we were thinking about having our wedding reception, I noticed that their menus and other printed materials looked dated and showed signs of age," a friend said. "I mentioned my work and asked if they'd consider reducing the price of our reception in exchange for some original, creative art-work and printing. They agreed, and we both walked away happy!"

Going Online for Services

Whether you live in Big City or Small Town, your life has been changed by the Internet. It's not only given us an information highway, it's provided merchants all over the world with more prospective customers for their goods and services. How can you find these goods and services without spending so much time online that you cause your fiancé, family, and friends to think you're addicted to that computer?

 FACT

Thousands of vendors offering goods and services abound on the Internet. Being very, very specific with your search will be the best way to find what you want without spending hours and hours at the computer.

Let Others Review for You

Many other brides and grooms have gone before you. So have those who have helped arrange weddings, or whose business is the business of weddings. Use their experience to help you find what you need without spending a lot of time and money in your efforts. Study the links on the wedding Web sites, and take a look at the Web sites some couples have posted for other couples to read what they learned about wedding planning.

Look Into It!

For information on everything you need to know about every aspect of planning a wedding, start with the wedding magazines and wedding vendors. Here's a list of some popular wedding Web sites:

> *www.theknot.com*
> *www.ModernBride.com*
> *www.TodaysBride.com*
> *www.MarthaStewart.com*
>   (click on "Wedding & Gift Registry")
> *www.Brides.com*
> *www.weddingexpressions.com*
> *www.ivillage.com*
> *www.wedfrugal.com*
> *www.blissweddings.com*
> *www.100.com*

Get Specific!

Getting specific about saving for your wedding? There are many Web sites offering coupons and rebates on wedding items (especially wedding-related Web sites). Also consider saving on everyday items with the aim in mind of putting aside those extra dollars you save for your wedding or honeymoon fund. One popular site is *www.coupon.com*.

ESSENTIAL

> The Dollar Stretcher newsletter, available on *www.stretcher.com*, is a great source of money-saving ideas and suggestions from cost-conscious writers and contributors.

Become an Educated Consumer

The better informed you are, the more money and time you'll save—not only on your wedding, but in every area of your life. Learning from the experiences of your friends and family as they navigated the wedding-planning highway can save you big bucks. Logging on to the Internet and scanning informational articles can be entertaining as well as informational. Comparison shopping and exploring other options can expand your understanding of what's available to you, whether you live in Big City or Small Town.

Take a Course!

Have you ever explored the many great classes, workshops, and seminars available in your area? Even the smallest of towns usually has some sort of educational institution available within a short driving distance. The cost can range from a nominal fee to hundreds of dollars, and some may even be free. You've probably taken courses you *had* to take for educational purposes or for training at your workplace. But have you ever taken a course simply to learn, have fun, and save money?

What about a course to learn to better budget your money? There can't be a better time than when you're planning for your wedding—and preparing for the life you'll have together with your fiancé. Just think how that budget class will pay off: in money savings, the ability to set and achieve realistic goals (like buying a home), and—best of all—fewer disagreements about money with your significant other.

Lessons for Wedding-Related Savings

What about taking a flower-arranging course, where you can learn how to make bouquets and centerpieces for your wedding? Maybe your mother or a friend would like to attend with you. How about a craft class to create unique invitations, or a computer class to learn how to create a wedding Web site (for more on this innovative idea, see Chapter 12)? Perhaps you and your fiancé would like to take a cooking class—whether it's to learn the basics, master some new techniques, or get an introduction to a new type of cuisine.

To find a class near you, check out your local adult education or community education departments, community colleges and four-year universities, county extension departments, YMCAs and YWCAs, and so on.

Classes on male/female relationships are fun to take together and will give you coping tools for your own relationship, too. Fitness or self-defense courses will make you stronger and better able to handle stress at this hectic time in your life.

Free Prenup Advice

You might not believe this, but prenuptials can be romantic. And they can save you money. Why? Because marriage is a business relationship as well as a romantic one. Neither of you should lose your belongings, good credit, and so on, if something ever goes wrong and you decide to separate. Right now, while you're in love and want the best for each other, is when some experts feel you should be deciding how things will be if that day ever comes. And it's not just celebrities and people with lots of money that need prenuptial agreements.

 FACT

Financial expert Suze Orman talks about prenuptials and how they're in the best interests of modern couples in her books and on her Web site, ✑*www.suzeorman.com.*

Not talking about the need for a prenuptial agreement won't keep the reason you need one from happening. But avoiding it will cost you big later on! Don't be too scared to talk about this with your fiancé. And let's hope that once you draw up the agreement, you will never have to see it again!

Sample Budget Worksheet

Use this handy worksheet to document expenses for your wedding. Keeping track of everything you spend will ensure that you stay within your budget. You might want to make a copy of the worksheet and tuck it into your purse or daily calendar so you remember to make entries as soon as you make the purchases. Feel free to customize this worksheet a bit, depending on your particular wedding plans.

BUDGET WORKSHEET

Wedding consultant
(if using one): $ _____

Ceremony site fee: $ _____

Reception site food
and beverages: $ _____

Wedding cake: $ _____

Cake knife, cake stand,
and other utensils: $ _____

Clothing for the bride:

    Dress: $ _____

    Headpiece: $ _____

    Shoes: $ _____

    Undergarments
    and pantyhose: $ _____

    Hairdresser
    and makeup: $ _____

Clothing for the groom:

    Tux rental or purchase: $ _____

    Shoes: $ _____

continued on page 249

BUDGET WORKSHEET

Clothing for the groom: (*continued*)

Underwear and socks: $ _ _ _ _ _ _ _ _ _ _ _ _ _

Stationery and postage:

Save-the-date cards: $ _ _ _ _ _ _ _ _ _ _ _ _ _

Invitations: $ _ _ _ _ _ _ _ _ _ _ _ _ _

Thank-you cards: $ _ _ _ _ _ _ _ _ _ _ _ _ _

Programs: $ _ _ _ _ _ _ _ _ _ _ _ _ _

Postage: $ _ _ _ _ _ _ _ _ _ _ _ _ _

Flowers:

Bridal bouquet: $ _ _ _ _ _ _ _ _ _ _ _ _ _

Attendants' bouquets: $ _ _ _ _ _ _ _ _ _ _ _ _ _

Corsages and
boutonnieres: $ _ _ _ _ _ _ _ _ _ _ _ _ _

Ceremony site flowers
and decorations: $ _ _ _ _ _ _ _ _ _ _ _ _ _

Reception site flowers
and decorations: $ _ _ _ _ _ _ _ _ _ _ _ _ _

Miscellaneous flowers
and decorations: $ _ _ _ _ _ _ _ _ _ _ _ _ _

continued on page 251

BUDGET WORKSHEET

Music:

    Ceremony site music: $ _____

    Reception site music: $ _____

Transportation: $ _____

Photography: $ _____

Videography: $ _____

Wedding favors
    and frills: $ _____

Wedding party gifts: $ _____

Tips: $ _____

Fees:

    Officiant: $ _____

    Marriage license: $ _____

    Blood tests, etc.: $ _____

Wedding insurance: $ _____

Wedding party expenses
(if you're paying hotel,
    airfare, etc.): $ _____

Wedding Web site: $ _____

continued on page 253

BUDGET WORKSHEET

Entertainment expenses
(for out-of-town
   guests, etc.): $ _____

Engagement dinner: $ _____

Rehearsal dinner: $ _____

Honeymoon:

   Airfare: $ _____

   Car rental: $ _____

   Accommodations: $ _____

   Food: $ _____

   Entertainment: $ _____

   Travel insurance: $ _____

Miscellaneous:

_____: $ _____

_____: $ _____

_____: $ _____

_____: $ _____

_____: $ _____

TOTAL: $ _____

Appendix B

Time Budget Worksheet

Many people will tell you to begin planning your wedding a year in advance. If that time frame will be shorter for you, don't panic! Just move the steps up as you need to, delegate, and set your priorities from the start!

TIME BUDGET WORKSHEET

TO DO	DATE DONE/DEPOSIT MADE/ FINAL PAYMENT MADE
Set the date	-------------
Decide on number of guests	-------------
Set budget	-------------
Reserve ceremony site	-------------
Reserve reception site	-------------
Hire wedding consultant (if desired)	-------------
Arrange for a wedding officiant	-------------
Order wedding and other invitations	-------------
Mail wedding and other invitations	-------------
Order or buy wedding dress and accessories	-------------
Order or buy tuxes and accessories	-------------
Order or buy bridesmaids' dresses	-------------

continued on page 259

TIME BUDGET WORKSHEET

TO DO	DATE DONE/DEPOSIT MADE/ FINAL PAYMENT MADE
Take care of dress alterations	_____
Put deposit down on flowers	_____
Put deposit down on cake	_____
Put deposit down on catering	_____
Put deposit down on music	_____
Put deposit down on transportation	_____
Put deposit down on photographer	_____
Put deposit down on videographer	_____
Put deposit down on rental items	_____
Get blood tests and license, etc.	_____

continued on page 261

TIME BUDGET WORKSHEET

TO DO	DATE DONE/DEPOSIT MADE/ FINAL PAYMENT MADE
Make hair and makeup appointment	_____
Buy wedding rings	_____
Buy/make wedding favors	_____
Buy wedding party gifts and other gifts	_____
Plan the engagement party	_____
Plan rehearsal dinner	_____
Plan other functions, such as brunch	_____
Plan honeymoon	_____
Make reservations and travel plans	_____
Get wedding insurance	_____
Get travel insurance	_____
Schedule a break for bride and groom before ceremony	_____

Index

We Have EVERYTHING!

Everything® **After College Book**

Everything® **American History Book**

Everything® **Angels Book**

Everything® **Anti-Aging Book**

Everything® **Astrology Book**

Everything® **Astronomy Book**

Everything® **Baby Names Book**

Everything® **Baby Shower Book**

Everything® **Baby's First Food Book**

Everything® **Baby's First Year Book**

Everything® **Barbecue Cookbook**

Everything® **Bartender's Book**

Everything® **Bedtime Story Book**

Everything® **Bible Stories Book**

Everything® **Bicycle Book**

Everything® **Breastfeeding Book**

Everything® **Budgeting Book**

Everything® **Build Your Own Home Page Book**

Everything® **Business Planning Book**

Everything® **Candlemaking Book**

Everything® **Car Care Book**

Everything® **Casino Gambling Book**

Everything® **Cat Book**

Everything® **Chocolate Cookbook**

Everything® **Christmas Book**

Everything® **Civil War Book**

Everything® **Classical Mythology Book**

Everything® **Coaching and Mentoring Book**

Everything® **Collectibles Book**

Everything® **College Survival Book**

Everything® **Computer Book**

Everything® **Cookbook**

Everything® **Cover Letter Book**

Everything® **Creative Writing Book**

Everything® **Crossword and Puzzle Book**

Everything® **Dating Book**

Everything® **Dessert Cookbook**

Everything® **Diabetes Cookbook**

Everything® **Dieting Book**

Everything® **Digital Photography Book**

Everything® **Dog Book**

Everything® **Dog Training and Tricks Book**

Everything® **Dreams Book**

Everything® **Etiquette Book**

Everything® **Fairy Tales Book**

Everything® **Family Tree Book**

Everything® **Feng Shui Book**

Everything® **Fly-Fishing Book**

Everything® **Games Book**

Everything® **Get-A-Job Book**

Everything® **Get Out of Debt Book**

Everything® **Get Published Book**

Everything® **Get Ready for Baby Book**

Everything® **Get Rich Book**

Everything® **Ghost Book**

Everything® **Golf Book**

Everything® **Grammar and Style Book**

Everything® **Great Thinkers Book**

Everything® **Guide to Las Vegas**

Everything® **Guide to New England**

Everything® **Guide to New York City**

Everything® **Travel Guide to The Disneyland Resort®, California Adventure®, Universal Studios®, and the Anaheim Area**

Everything® **Travel Guide to Walt Disney World®, Universal Studios®, and Greater Orlando, 3rd Ed.**

Everything® **Guide to Washington D.C.**

Everything® **Guide to Writing Children's Books**

Everything® **Guitar Book**

Everything® **Herbal Remedies Book**

Everything® **Home-Based Business Book**

Everything® **Homebuying Book**

Everything® **Homeselling Book**

Everything® **Horse Book**

Everything® **Hot Careers Book**

Everything® **Hypnosis Book**

To order, call 1-800-872-5627 or visit everything.com!

Everything® **Internet Book**

Everything® **Investing Book**

Everything® **Jewish Wedding Book**

Everything® **Judaism Book**

Everything® **Job Interview Book**

Everything® **Knitting Book**

Everything® **Lawn Care Book**

Everything® **Leadership Book**

Everything® **Learning French Book**

Everything® **Learning Italian Book**

Everything® **Learning Spanish Book**

Everything® **Low-Carb Cookbook**

Everything® **Low-Fat High-Flavor Cookbook**

Everything® **Magic Book**

Everything® **Managing People Book**

Everything® **Meditation Book**

Everything® **Menopause Book**

Everything® **Microsoft® Word 2000 Book**

Everything® **Money Book**

Everything® **Mother Goose Book**

Everything® **Motorcycle Book**

Everything® **Mutual Funds Book**

Everything® **Network Marketing Book**

Everything® **Numerology Book**

Everything® **One-Pot Cookbook**

Everything® **Online Business Book**

Everything® **Online Genealogy Book**

Everything® **Online Investing Book**

Everything® **Online Job Search Book**

Everything® **Organize Your Home Book**

Everything® **Pasta Book**

Everything® **Philosophy Book**

Everything® **Pilates Book**

Everything® **Playing Piano and Keyboards Book**

Everything® **Potty Training Book**

Everything® **Pregnancy Book**

Everything® **Pregnancy Organizer**

Everything® **Project Management Book**

Everything® **Puppy Book**

Everything® **Quick Meals Cookbook**

Everything® **Resume Book**

Everything® **Romance Book**

Everything® **Running Book**

Everything® **Sailing Book, 2nd Ed.**

Everything® **Saints Book**

Everything® **Scrapbooking Book**

Everything® **Selling Book**

Everything® **Shakespeare Book**

Everything® **Slow Cooker Cookbook**

Everything® **Soup Cookbook**

Everything® **Spells and Charms Book**

Everything® **Start Your Own Business Book**

Everything® **Stress Management Book**

Everything® **Study Book**

Everything® **T'ai Chi and QiGong Book**

Everything® **Tall Tales, Legends, and Other Outrageous Lies Book**

Everything® **Tarot Book**

Everything® **Thai Cookbook**

Everything® **Time Management Book**

Everything® **Toasts Book**

Everything® **Toddler Book**

Everything® **Total Fitness Book**

Everything® **Trivia Book**

Everything® **Tropical Fish Book**

Everything® **Vegetarian Cookbook**

Everything® **Vitamins, Minerals, and Nutritional Supplements Book**

Everything® **Weather Book**

Everything® **Wedding Book, 2nd Ed.**

Everything® **Wedding Checklist**

Everything® **Wedding Etiquette Book**

Everything® **Wedding Organizer**

Everything® **Wedding Shower Book**

Everything® **Wedding Vows Book**

Everything® **Weddings on a Budget Book**

Everything® **Weight Training Book**

Everything® **Wicca and Witchcraft Book**

Everything® **Wine Book**

Everything® **World War II Book**

Everything® **World's Religions Book**

Everything® **Yoga Book**

We Have
EVERYTHING®
For Weddings!

The Everything Wedding Book, Third Edition

Trade paperback
1-59337-126-8, $14.95

The Everything Wedding Organizer

Trade paperback, spiral bound
1-55850-828-7, $15.00

Trade paperback
1-58062-456-1, $7.95

Trade paperback
1-58062-454-5, $7.95

Trade paperback
1-58062-455-3, $9.95

Trade paperback
1-58062-188-0, $7.95